Hurt, Healing, and Happy Again

Martin Weber

REVIEW AND HERALD® PUBLISHING ASSOCIATION
WASHINGTON, DC 20039-0555
HAGERSTOWN, MD 21740

Copyright © 1989 by
Review and Herald® Publishing Association

This book was
Edited by Gerald Wheeler
Designed by Bill Kirstein

Type set: 9.9 pt Garamond Book

Printed in U.S.A.

R&H Cataloging Service

Weber, Martin Herbert, 1951-
    Hurt, healing, and happy again.

    1. Loneliness.   2. Spiritual life.   I. Title.
                248

ISBN 0-8280-0531-1

Introduction

All the Lonely People . . .

A lonely young drifter crossed the country in a bus. Nobody greeted him at the Greyhound terminal in Washington. Nobody accompanied him as he prowled around the rain-soaked streets near the White House. And nobody spoke to him as he fidgeted among the crowd outside the Hilton Hotel.

Then six sudden shots immortalized the name of John Hinckley. We almost lost our president as the lonesome gunman tried to prove his love for Jodie Foster, the teenage actress he idolized. His bizarre plot availed him nothing, however. Nothing but confinement—deeper solitude than before.

Few of us would resort to assassination to solve the problem of loneliness. Yet despite our dismay at Hinckley's crime, millions can identify with his emotional isolation. We share his burning yearning to be wanted, needed, understood by somebody special. Empty hearts are screaming, "I've been cheated and mistreated—when will I be loved?" No less than teen idol Michael Jackson lamented in his recent book, "I must be the loneliest person in the world." Evidently popularity in itself can't satisfy a lonely heart.

Years ago the Beatles recorded a mournful song with the haunting questions "All the lonely people, where do they all come from? All the lonely people, where do they all belong?"

Lonely people don't belong to anyone, it seems.

Alice,* a widow in her 70s, raised five children on a dairy farm in Ohio. Three of them moved long distances away, and the two who live nearby don't visit much. She thinks about them day and night, gazing fondly at their pictures, hoping that tomorrow's mail will bring a letter. But between Mother's Day and Christmas Alice's children don't seem to know she exists. In her darkest hours she wonders if they might be waiting for her to die so they can grab their share of her hard-earned savings.

Her youngest son, Jack, used to have a family and a job. Now his only companions are the dozens of broken brown bottles he sleeps beside under a railroad bridge. Jack calls his brokenhearted mother (collect) now and then when he needs drinking money. His shattered life may be his own fault, but guilt won't help him now.

Shari has the apartment down the hall from Alice. She used to be a popular cheerleader in high school. Fellow classmates had selected her as the one among them "most likely to succeed." Unfortunately, Shari's quest for a career left no time to nurture her relationships. Now in her late 30s, she's all alone. Time is passing her by, and her good looks are fading fast.

Shari and Jack and Alice are symbols of single people who suffer intense loneliness. But millions of married people also live in emotional exile. John, an accountant who works with Shari, feels let down by his wife, Linda. She criticizes him for failing to communicate and blames him for being a workaholic—yet she welcomes every dollar he earns from his overtime hours. Her attitude frustrates and embitters him.

Linda herself seethes with resentment. Motherhood appears to require a 20-year sentence of solitary confinement within the walls of her house. Naturally, Linda adores her twin toddlers, but she craves adult relationships, too. Daytime game shows and soap operas offer familiar faces but only counterfeit companionship.

It's a big mess, this business of loneliness. All the lonely people—where do they all belong?

In church, perhaps. Unfortunately, religion with its rules and its rigid reverence often fails to fill the empty heart. God seems too holy and too high in the sky to offer much companionship for lonely people.

But we might do well to take another look within the covers of the Bible. In those sacred pages we discover that our Omnipotent God is also a tender Father. And believe it or not, He is lonesome up there. Hungering for human companionship, He yearns for every wandering prodigal to come home to His heart.

Lonely people belong in the arms of God. In these pages we will explore how to master the possibilities of a relationship with Him.

------

* Except for famous personalities, I have changed names to preserve privacy. All cases in this book depict actual experiences. Individual names may represent a composite of the lives of several people, however.

Chapter 1

Jeff Survives an Affair

When Jeff saw Angela, it was love at first sight. No doubt about it, they made the perfect match.

There was just one problem. Both of them were already married.

The affair began quite innocently. Angela met Jeff in the waiting room outside a chaplain's office—of all places. She had come for counseling to cope with her loneliness. Her husband, a Navy man off at sea, wouldn't be home for four months.

Four months of solitude in a strange city! If only she had a friend to help her pass the time. That's when Jeff entered her life. Such a caring, sensitive Christian brother—a gift sent by God, she felt sure.

Jeff was lonely too, since his job had moved him across the country from his wife. He too felt that his prayers had been answered.

Every evening that first week they phoned each other to pray together and talk about the day's events. The bond between them strengthened. Pure Christian friendship, no doubt.

Another week flew by as their loneliness vanished. Angela looked forward to her husband coming home and meeting Jeff. The three of them would be great pals, doing things together.

Then one evening Angela invited Jeff to her apartment for supper. Nothing fancy, just a simple meal to enjoy their simple friendship. It started raining, so he stayed longer than he intended. After all, how could he ride his motorcycle home on slick roads?

The 10:00 news came and went with the rain still pouring down. Now it was getting late. What should they do? Angela had an idea: "Jeff, why don't you just stay here overnight and sleep on the living room couch? That's what my brother does when he visits—and you're my brother too!"

No problem. A perfectly innocent solution.

How wonderful that evening to pray together in person rather than over the phone. They got up from their knees and said good night. He sat down on the couch, yawned, and went to sleep.

The next morning he awoke to find Angela sitting next to him, asleep against his arm. The morning sunlight gilded her tousled blonde curls. He noticed her cute nose, those delicate lips, her slender body. For the first time he admitted to himself that she was pretty.

In fact, she was gorgeous! Why try to deny it any longer?

His mind started wondering . . . maybe the Lord wanted them to experience a new dimension in their friendship. A special closeness.

That afternoon after work he took her to the park for a walk. They tossed bread to the ducks, laughing at the antics of God's feathered creatures. Halfway around the lake she noticed that he had become quiet. His hand reached for hers. It was the first time he had touched her.

"I don't know if I should be telling you this," he ventured, "but this morning when I woke up and found you sitting next to me asleep, you looked so sweet and precious. I noticed how lovely you are, and I—I almost asked if I could kiss you."

Her blue eyes met his. Several tantalizing seconds passed. Then she squeezed his hand and whispered, "Why didn't you?"

That evening after dinner, you can imagine what happened. Jeff and Angela did kiss. Then they fell into each other's arms and became lovers.

The next several months they lived together in a fantasy paradise. Jeff told me about it when I visited him on one of my trips back East. We sat on the rug in his living room as he reminisced.

"Never before in my life had I enjoyed such a relationship. You wouldn't believe the pleasures we shared together. Heaven on earth."

"I'm not sure you know this," I responded, "but while you lived in 'heaven' with Angela, your wife suffered an emotional hell. She visited our home to cry on our shoulders. And that little girl of yours kept asking, 'Where's Daddy?'"

He stared down at the floor as we sat silently for a while. Then the doorbell rang with the pizza we had ordered. Jeff offered a quick prayer and we started eating. He continued his story.

"You know, I've gone through hell myself over this. When Angela's husband came home, the party was over. It had to end sooner or later, I guess. All I had left were memories. Emotional ashes.

"Without her the world seemed so cruel. For a long time it was unbearable! I felt like shouting at the cars passing by my apartment, 'Don't you care?' Every night I cried my heart out."

Jeff paused and wiped a tear before he could go on.

"I missed Angela so much, but what could I do? She didn't belong to me. Her husband didn't deserve to lose his wife. I tried moving back home to my own wife in California. We did our best to work it out, but we ended up divorcing.

"So there I was, alone again. I had to find someone new. That's how I met Darcy. She's beautiful, and who knows, I might marry her someday. But I'll never get Angela out of my mind. Not as long as I live."

Jeff gave me permission to tell you his experience. As usual, I'm changing names and circumstances to protect their privacy.

The relationship he had with Angela certainly isn't unique. Adultery has become a national epidemic. In recent times women have been unfaithful to their husbands as never before. As for men, some surveys indicate that in some states more men cheat than vote!

While the situation is shocking indeed, and extremely sad, it is not hopeless. One can find hope and help in Jesus to survive an affair, as Jeff discovered the evening of my visit.

I first knew Jeff back in the late seventies. He and his wife had been deeply in love, always holding hands and hugging. But somehow, after several years holy wedlock became unhappy deadlock. Jeff didn't care when his career moved him away from home across the country. His wife felt reluctant to join him, so he settled into his new job by himself. Before long he found himself intensely lonely, emotionally hungry for that affair with Angela.

Looking back now, he admitted that he and Angela had not been living in reality. The thrill of romance sugarcoated the stresses and strains of normal life—things like overdue bills, dental appointments, cars breaking down. But sooner or later the passion had to wear off, exposing their unresolved problems.

An affair that soars through the summer often flutters down to earth with autumn's leaves. I've noticed it usually takes between three and six months for illicit lovers to break up. So Jeff and Angela were probably due anyway for a big letdown about the time her husband returned home.

But as it was, he had nothing but good times while he lived with her. "We shared a lot of love," he recalled wistfully. "To this day I couldn't say our affair was sinful. We didn't have a pornographic relationship—I didn't lust after Angela's body. It was tender, giving love. A beautiful foretaste of what heaven will be like."

At this point I needed to confront Jeff with spiritual reality. "But what makes you so sure you will be in heaven?

The Bible warns, 'There is a way which seems right to a man, but its end is the way of death' (Proverbs 14:12). Adultery may seem OK, but it ends in death. The death of your home. The death of your self-respect. And unless you repent, Jeff, even the death of your soul."

He didn't mind my talking to him like a Dutch uncle, so I continued.

"You say you had a 'giving' type of relationship with Angela. But really, weren't you being selfish? Taking away from your wife and your daughter, robbing them of a husband and father? And what about Angela's husband?"

It was tough medicine for him, sitting there sipping his 7-Up. He was listening, though. I kept on:

"The Bible says there's nothing so self-destructive and self-deceptive as the human heart. We can rationalize almost anything. Temptations from Satan appear to be blessings from God. Things immoral and selfish seem wonderful, even desirable."

Jeff hadn't considered any of this. He wanted to hear more.

"Visit a dairy farm, and inside the barn you see flies buzzing around the floor behind the cows. What's the big attraction down there?"

My friend grinned. He got the point as I pressed it further:

"Because of our sinful nature, we have the same problem as those flies in the barn. Immoral sex attracts us, but just because sin feels right—does that make it right?

"Suppose you went outdoors tonight in that freezing weather. If you got cold enough, you might enjoy having a bucket of warm water dumped on you. It would feel good at first. But soon you would be frozen stiff, in worse shape than before!"

Jeff nodded thoughtfully. His experience with Angela had taught him one of life's important lessons—often our solutions bring us more trouble than the problems we want them to take care of.

Well, my little sermon had gotten through to him, thank God. Leaning back with a sigh, he said, "That affair was fun, all right, but I see now that it was wrong. Angela and I hurt our families and we hurt ourselves. Although we thought we were solving our loneliness problem, we ended up more miserable than if we had never been friends. We wrecked our lives with selfishness and sin."

Adultery doesn't solve problems—it compounds them. It's not an oasis of happiness but a mirage, unable to quench the thirst for lasting love.

Poor Jeff sat there looking sad. But now that he admitted his sin problem (something all of us equally share), he could appreciate the good news about a Saviour who forgives us, heals our hurts, and guides us into God's special plan for our lives.

The two of us shoved aside our half-eaten pizza and reached for our Bibles. Jeff had been neglecting the Scriptures for many years, but now he was eager to get into the Word again. We studied about God's great love for sinners, how He sent Jesus to this world to pay the price of our salvation. And what a price it was—death on the cross. Crucifixion was the most dragged-out, painful, and shameful way a criminal could die in the ancient world.

First the executioners stripped the victim. Then they spiked his feet through the heel bones with huge nails. After that, they stretched his arms and bound and nailed them to the crossbar, so that the weight of the victim's body would nearly suffocate him. He had to push himself up each time he needed to breathe. All this happened in front of a hooting, howling mob that mocked the dying agonies of the naked criminal.

Our Lord hung on the cross in open humiliation. No wonder the women stood off in the distance at Calvary (Matthew 27:55). We can see why the New Testament speaks so often of the shame of the cross.

The night before His crucifixion Jesus withdrew for prayer to the Garden of Gethsemane. A strange and deadly despair began suffocating Him. It wasn't the pain and the shame that weighed most heavily on His heart, but a special kind of loneliness. You see, His Father would have to forsake Him on the cross in order to accept repenting sinners.

Jesus shrank in horror from the ordeal. Bloody sweat poured down His brow as He cried, "Father, if it's possible to save sinners without My going through that hell, please take this cup of suffering away!"

However, it wasn't possible for Jesus to escape the cross and still rescue us from sin. Thus, despite His strange and awful loneliness, He decided to go through with His supreme sacrifice. And so "He was pierced through for our transgressions, He was crushed for our iniquities: The chastening for our well-being fell upon Him, and by His scourging we are healed. All of us like sheep have gone astray. Each of us has turned to his own way; But the Lord has caused the iniquity of us all to fall on Him" (Isaiah 53:5, 6, NASB).

God treated Jesus as we deserve so that we might be treated as He deserves. He wore our crown of thorns so that we could wear His crown of glory. Jesus suffered our death so that we might receive His life—eternal life with Him in heaven.

As Jeff and I pondered these wonderful possibilities, his eyes brightened with hope. Hope for forgiveness, cleansing, new life in Jesus. Then I told him about another man who by God's grace had survived an affair. Long ago in ancient Jerusalem King David from his palace rooftop noticed a woman bathing. Dazzled by her beauty, he arranged a secret rendezvous. The woman, named Bathsheba, became pregnant.

Rather than confess and come clean of his scandal, David attempted a royal cover-up. He arranged the secret murder of Bathsheba's husband. Then he whisked the beautiful widow to his palace so they could live happily ever after. Nobody would know what had happened.

Nobody, that is, but God. He dispatched His prophet to confront the wayward ruler.

David repented. Psalm 51 records his sobs of confession:

"Have mercy on me, O God, according to your unfailing love; according to your great compassion. . . . Wash away all my iniquity and cleanse me from my sin" (verses 1, 2, NIV).

From the depths of his broken heart the adulterous king cried for mercy and forgiveness. And he craved more: "Create in me a pure heart, O God" (verse 10, NASB).

God heard his plea and forgave him fully. He gave David and Bathsheba a new life, even blessing their marriage with a son who reigned on David's throne. You may know that the family tree of Jesus Christ includes David, Bathsheba, and their son Solomon. Read it for yourself in Matthew 1.

What was God doing, adopting David and Bathsheba into His family tree—and then broadcasting the startling fact in the first chapter of the New Testament? He wants us to know that He can also forgive you and me and restore us to respectability.

Jeff concluded that if God had pardoned and restored David, He could do the same for him. But that does not mean that there wouldn't be any more pain. Although God forgave the repenting king, some people couldn't. David suffered the scars of his sin as long as he lived. And his sons followed his immoral example and brought ruin upon the royal family. Yet through all the tough times God stayed with David, comforting and strengthening him.

My friend knew he would also suffer permanent damage from his fling with Angela. But with God's forgiveness and strength, life would be bearable, even enjoyable, again.

By now it was nearly 2:00 in the morning. Jeff had to be at work by 7:00, and I had to get up early to catch a plane home. As we prayed together—a very special prayer—he gave his heart to Jesus.

Although I haven't heard from Jeff lately, I know God is with him, lavishing him with heaven's unrelenting love. I hope he always follows the Lord's plan for his life.

And you who are reading this—God loves you just as much as He does Jeff or anyone else. Have you been looking for love in all the wrong places? You may be so disappointed, so disgusted with yourself that you can't stand the face in your mirror. But take courage. Sinful though we are, we may come boldly to our God for mercy. There's plenty enough forgiveness in His loving heart to bury every one of our sins!

Calvary brings us the glorious promise: "If we confess our sins, he is faithful and just and will forgive us our sins and purify us from all unrighteousness" (1 John 1:9, NIV).

Does that sound like good news to you? Too good to pass up, wouldn't you say?

And Jesus offers more than forgiveness. He helps us untangle our relationships. He restores us to responsible, respectable living.

Are you struggling with temptation? Jesus understands. Come boldly to Him for strength. Our next chapter will discuss how to cope with temptation and experience victory.

But maybe you don't want victory over sin just yet. Despite the guilt involved, your affair has been so intoxicating you don't feel like sobering up now. Perhaps later. Well, just remember that living in sin is living a lie. The time for truth will always come—and the sooner the better.

Nothing melts selfishness and stubbornness like thoughts centered on Jesus. Our sins broke His heart on the cross. Once we realize what they cost the Saviour, sinning can never be the same. Calvary's love draws us toward repentance. Why resist?

Suppose now that you have decided to repent of your affair. You know God forgives you, but your spouse holds a grudge. Or maybe you still feel more affection for your ex-lover than for the partner you betrayed. Flashbacks keep coming back from your illicit relationship. God understands your silent grief.

Although you may not see any reason for hope, God can heal your heart and your home. Even though you may not feel like it, invest your emotional energies into your marriage. Put your fantasies to work surprising your spouse. Plan special times of closeness away from the rat race. And believe it or not, the excitement may someday return to your relationship.

Meanwhile, let your emotional hunger pull you into the closest possible relationship with Jesus. He's always there to lavish your heart with His love and satisfy your deepest needs.

Perhaps you have been reading this chapter from the outside looking in—you are the victim of your spouse's affair. Consequently you wonder what to do about the whole big mess. Well, the Bible does allow divorce in cases of adultery. But if your partner is willing to work to restore the former relationship, wouldn't it be better to save your home?

Possibly you could have been more warm and loving to your spouse. Who knows, that might have prevented the affair. Adultery has no excuse, of course, under any circumstances. But all of us can think back and see how we could have been better husbands and wives.

Maybe you aren't ready to forgive your spouse. The wounds are just too deep, leaving you with too much resentment. Remember that God has forgiven your sins. Do we now have the right to withhold forgiveness from a fellow sinner?

If you don't feel like forgiving your partner's affair, it might help to know that forgiveness isn't a feeling. Love itself involves more than emotion. Mother may not feel like jumping out of bed at midnight to nurse a sick child, but love makes her do it anyway. And consider Calvary. Jesus had no longing to get Himself nailed to the cross, yet that sacrifice was the greatest loving act of all time.

Being "in love"—what does it mean? Many couples divorce because they think they have fallen out of love. They've lost that loving feeling, so they imagine they can't go on together.

How mistaken we can be! We can choose to love if we want to. God will help us. You might also need the help of a Christian counselor to save your marriage. Whatever it takes, why not do it now?

Suppose it's already too late to salvage your marriage. It was that way for Jeff. His former wife met a nice Christian fellow and they formed a new home. Although Jeff couldn't resurrect his former marriage, he could survive his affair by accepting new life in Jesus. And thank the Lord, he did.

God is the God of new beginnings. When we entrust our ruined lives to His care, He forgives our sins, heals our broken hearts, and brings harmony out of confusion.

Can we possibly resist responding to such love?

If you want more:

    Psalm 32
    Proverbs 28:13
    Isaiah 55:6, 7
    Romans 8:28, 31-39

Chapter 2

David's Narrow Escape

O f all the exciting people I've met, none can compare with David.

He was a decorated war hero, talented musician and poet with deep spiritual insight, and the handsome heartthrob of the nation's women.

You would think anyone would be proud to claim such a fine young man for a relative. But no, his wife's father grew so jealous of his popularity that he tried to murder him. David had to escape through a back window to the wilderness, where his father-in-law tried to hunt him down.

Sound incredible? We find all this and more about David in the Bible. Although he lived 3,000 years ago, his amazing adventures rivet one's attention as much as anything from Hollywood.

Scripture tells us more about David than his life story. Many of the psalms, a collection of musical poetry, preserve a diary of his inner turmoil—joy and sorrow, faith and frustration. Millions of Christians and Jewish people begin each morning in prayer with the Psalms, finding in them encouragement and strength.

In this chapter I'll introduce some of my favorite psalms and the particular experiences that David had that inspired them. I hope you will see the possibilities for you to enjoy a fulfilling friendship with God, as David did.

First, let's get acquainted with David's background. The youngest of eight sons, he lived in Bethlehem (birthplace of Jesus Christ 1,000 years later). Growing up tending sheep on the peaceful hills outside town, David learned lessons there that prepared him for a sudden and dramatic change in his life.

One day the prophet Samuel showed up and selected the astonished teenager to be Israel's future king. The reigning monarch, Saul, had plunged the nation toward spiritual bankruptcy, so the Lord told Samuel to anoint young David as its next leader.

But how could a teenager dethrone a powerful king? Well, God can be quite creative in working out His plan for our lives. Through an unlikely chain of providences the shepherd boy found himself thrust into the national political arena.

The Philistines, Israel's archenemies, staged an invasion. David's brothers went off to battle while he stayed home with his sheep. Later, while visiting his brothers to bring supplies, he encountered Goliath. As David heard the giant taunting the Israelite army and blaspheming God, his heart throbbed with righteous indignation. He loaded up his slingshot—and you know what happened next.

Instantly the young man became a national hero. "The women sang as they danced, and said, 'Saul has slain his thousands, and David his ten thousands'" (1 Samuel 18:7). Naturally, King Saul didn't appreciate second billing behind the slingshot kid. Raging with jealousy, he hurled his spear at David. When the young man escaped that unhealthy situation, Saul devised a sinister plot. Noting that his beautiful daughter had fallen in love with the new national hero, Saul offered her in marriage to his enemy. Here was the catch—David first had to kill 100 Philistine soldiers. Saul felt sure that his rival would not survive such a mission impossible.

But no, God blessed David and he killed a double number of Philistines. Saul had no choice but to make his enemy his son-in-law. Humiliated and furious, he sent soldiers to the newlyweds' house to murder David. The bride hurried her husband out the window, and he escaped to the wilderness.

Poor David, God's promise to make him king must have seemed farfetched. There in hiding, he confided to a friend, "As the Lord lives and as your soul lives, there is but a step between me and death" (1 Samuel 20:3).

Have you ever lived with just a step between you and death? Perhaps the death of your marriage or some other cherished relationship. Maybe the death of your finances. The loss of that once-in-a-lifetime opportunity. In his crisis hour David turned to His friend in heaven for help: "Deliver me from my enemies, O my God; defend me from those who rise up against me. . . . Awake to help me" (Psalm 59:1-4).

Then his desperation gave way to triumphant faith: "I will sing of Your power; yes, I will sing aloud of Your mercy in the morning; for You have been my defense and refuge in the day of my trouble" (verse 16).

Whatever our situation, we too can find refuge in God's mercy. In our darkest hour we can stretch our faith to the Lord and even sing about His power to save us!

However, David's troubles were far from over. The citizens of a city he had rescued from the Philistines were willing to betray him into Saul's hand. Talk about gratitude! David had to hit the road again.

Maybe you know the feeling. Have you ever risked yourself in helping someone, only to have that person turn against you? Saul, even while seeking to murder David, self-righteously declared to his accomplices: "Blessed are you of the Lord, for you have compassion on me" (1 Samuel 23:21).

No, things didn't look well for David. He poured out his heart to God in words captured by Psalm 54:1: "Save me, O God, by Your name, and vindicate me by Your strength." Recalling how God had delivered him so far, he took courage and exulted, "Behold, God is my helper; the Lord is with those who uphold my life" (verse 4).

He even claimed the promised deliverance as already reality: "I will praise Your name, O Lord, for it is good. For He has delivered me out of all trouble; and my eye has seen its desire upon my enemies" (verses 6, 7).

I'd call that faith, wouldn't you?

Despite his remarkable trust in God, David felt terribly lonely there in the wilderness, cut off from his wife and loved ones. In his solitude he lamented: "I lie awake, and am like a sparrow alone on the housetop" (Psalm 102:7).

Yet through it all, God sustained him. In his lonely hideout David composed one of the most sublime psalms, the sixty-third:

"O God, You are my God; early will I seek You; my soul thirsts for You; my flesh longs for You in a dry and thirsty land where there is no water. . . . Because Your lovingkindness is better than life, my lips shall praise You. . . . My soul shall be satisfied . . . , and my mouth shall praise You with joyful lips" (verses 1-5).

The lesson for us is clear—whatever our circumstances, we too can enjoy a satisfying relationship with God.

Let's not get confused, though. Despite David's deep love for God, he wasn't some kind of spiritual superman. Increasingly desperate as the crisis with Saul dragged on, he told a lie to the priest in order to obtain supplies. Saul accused the unsuspecting spiritual leader of treason for helping his enemy and then murdered 85 priests, plus the entire town of Nob—even the nursing babies.

Probably all of us through falsehood or misrepresentation have hurt people we love. We can understand how devastated David felt about what happened. As a consequence he fled to the Philistia, of all places, for refuge with his mortal enemies.

There he discovered to his horror that his reputation as a giant killer had preceded him. Terrified, David took drastic action to prove he wasn't a threat to them. "He changed his behavior before them, feigned madness in their hands, scratched on the doors of the gate, and let his saliva fall down on his beard" (1 Samuel 21:13).

Now we've all done foolish things under pressure. But few of us have resorted to antics quite like his. They worked, though. The Philistine king "Achish said to his servants, 'Look, you see the man is insane. Why have you brought him to me? Have I need of madmen, that you have brought this fellow to play the madman in my presence?'" (verses 14, 15). And so David in disgrace left Philistia to find some place more conducive to his physical and mental health.

Despite his madcap behavior there, David hadn't completely lost his mind about spiritual things. In gratitude for God's deliverance he composed one of his most eloquent psalms, the thirty-fourth:

"I sought the Lord, and He heard me, and delivered me from all my fears." (verse 4). "This poor man cried out, and the Lord heard him, and saved him out of all his troubles. The angel of the Lord encamps all around those who fear Him, and delivers them. Oh, taste and see that the Lord is good; blessed is the man who trusts in Him" (verses 6-8). "Many are the afflictions of the righteous, but the Lord delivers him out of them all" (verse 19).

Well, "David therefore departed from there and escaped to the cave of Adullam. . . . And everyone who was in distress, everyone who was in debt, and everyone who was discontented gathered to him. So he became captain over them. And there were about four hundred men with him" (1 Samuel 22:1, 2). David had his hands full bringing into line such a band of losers and malcontents.

If you are a parent, a teacher, or a leader of any kind, you might at times feel overwhelmed by the responsibility of those under your charge. But you can look to heaven for help, as David did, with these words:

"I cry out to the Lord with my voice; . . . I pour out my complaint before Him; I declare before Him my trouble. When my spirit was overwhelmed within me, then You knew my path" (Psalm 142:1-3).

Time and again David begins a psalm in total despair. Often he's afraid or sad. Sometimes he vents some terribly un-Christlike opinions about his enemies. That used to bother me, but now I realize such psalms have a purpose too. God wants to show us He can relate to struggling sinners no matter what mood we find ourselves in. Whether we feel mad, sad, bad, or glad, God loves us just the same and invites us to talk with Him.

Sometimes David got upset even at God, and at times he imagined God to be mad at him. But sooner or later in the psalm God managed to settle him down and fill his heart with praise and peace.

Years ago, I didn't feel comfortable talking with God when upset about something. I didn't consider myself spiritual enough to merit help from the Almighty. Now I know better—those are the times I need to pray the most. Unworthy though I am, I can always approach God with confidence through the blood of Jesus. Nothing prevents the mercy and power of God from reaching out to me under all circumstances. Isn't that encouraging?

When I first became a Christian back during college days, someone tried to help me by enforcing a rigid format in my prayers: always express adoration to God first, then thank Him for His blessings. Following that, confess sin. At last, after I had said and done all that, I could dare to discuss my needs with Him.

Some may find such a legalistic formula necessary. But don't you think it undermines our full and free fellowship with God? Often a problem weighs heavily on my mind, and I've got to get it out of the way first. Right now. Only then can I think clearly to praise God and adore Him.

We learn from the psalms that prayer requires no particular formula. What counts is that we keep ourselves honest with Him and open to His Spirit. Whenever conviction of sin comes to mind, confess it and flush away the guilt. Rejoice in forgiveness through Jesus Christ, then plan whatever arrangements possible to avoid yielding to temptation again.

A few years back I had the lofty goal of memorizing many of the psalms. The project isn't going well, I have to admit. Even so, I find that as long as I'm spending time in meaningful study, the Lord helps me recall those verses I need, even if I haven't memorized them.

I've read through the psalms a number of times, and now I'm doing it again. Usually a psalm every morning—sometimes less, sometimes more. When one of the verses particularly strikes a response in me, I talk to God about it. Maybe it's something sublime about God's mercy that echoes my feelings, and I pause to praise Him. Perhaps it's a promise I want to claim. Maybe I feel prompted to confess some shortcoming.

By mingling my reading of a psalm with prayer verse by verse, I can't run out of ideas to pray about. Usually after a few verses have gotten me started in prayer, I'll move on to talk with God about the challenges facing me that day and other things needing prayer.

If I have any time left, I'll turn to one of Paul's New Testament epistles for a few verses of practical instruction. Or I might go to the Gospels—Matthew, Mark, Luke, and John—to deepen my relationship with Jesus. Then I go jogging outside, and while huffing and puffing, I pray for people who need help.

That's my morning prayer habit. You may have another program that works for you. God made all of us different.

Now back to the adventures of David. There in the cave with his band of ruffians he composed Psalm 57:

"Be merciful to me, O God, be merciful to me! For my soul trusts in You; and in the shadow of Your wings I will make my refuge, until these calamities have passed by. I will cry out to God Most High, to God who performs all things for me" (verses 1, 2).

Again we see despair transformed to faith. Midnight in that dark cave turned to noontime with the sunlight of God's love.

Meanwhile, Saul got word that his enemy had abandoned Philistia and returned to Israel. The chase resumed, with 3,000 elite soldiers on David's trail. Humanly speaking, he didn't have a chance to survive. Yet somehow God carried him through crisis after crisis.

Things didn't seem to be getting better, though. David's future appeared bleaker than ever. Samuel, his beloved spiritual father, died. Then Saul gave David's wife to another man.

Forgetting to consult God for direction, David once again fled to his enemies in Philistia. There he landed a job as King Achish's bodyguard. (I assume he managed to convince the king he wasn't a maniac after all.) But this time he really got himself in hot water. The Philistines were planning to attack his homeland, and the king expected him to join the battle. But God had appointed David to be Israel's king. How could he raise his sword against them? Yet, as Achish's bodyguard, he had to march along with the Philistine army.

The dreaded day of battle came. David brought up the rear of the Philistine ranks, praying silently as hard as he could: "O God, get me out of this mess I've foolishly gotten myself into. Please, Lord!" Have you ever prayed like that? I've had to, hundreds of times, it seems.

Well, God did something special. He inspired the Philistine generals to protest David's presence among them, judging him unlikely to fight against his homeland. Faced with a possible revolt, Achish reluctantly dismissed David. Secretly delighted, David pretended to be offended that the Philistines didn't want him. Then he got out of there.

When David and his men returned once again to their homeland, they found a terrible calamity confronting them. A raiding band of Amalekites had burned their homes and kidnapped their wives and children. Nothing remained but ruins and ashes.

"Then David and the people who were with him lifted up their voices and wept, until they had no more power to weep." "David was greatly distressed, for the people spoke of stoning him, . . . But David strengthened himself in the Lord his God" (1 Samuel 30:4-6).

Once again in dire distress he put his hope in God. Leading his men after the raiders, they rescued their families unharmed and reclaimed their possessions.

After this crisis his wilderness wanderings finally ended. The Philistine invasion of Israel (after David left the army) led to Saul's death. The people demanded David for their new king.

At last God's promise had come to pass. Peace and power and prosperity entered the land. Blessed by God and popular with the people, David saw all his dreams come true. Then, just when everything was going perfectly, he made the most horrible mistake of his life. He committed his sin with Bathsheba, the affair and murder we discussed a few pages ago. Thankfully, he did repent. Psalm 51 records his contrition and recommitment.

Although the Lord fully and freely forgave David, irreversible damage remained. David lost the respect of the people, and his leadership languished. His own son Absalom launched a rebellion against him to take the throne, and David had to run for his life. He fled the royal city barefoot, his head covered in shame.

I don't know whether you've ever done anything like David did. If so you repented of your sin, God forgave you, but perhaps people didn't. Then you can relate to David's despair as he cried,

"Many are they who rise up against me. . . . But You, O Lord, are a shield for me, my glory and the One who lifts up my head. . . . I lay down and slept; I awoke, for the Lord sustained me. I will not be afraid of ten thousands of people who have set themselves against me all around" (Psalm 3:1-6).

God heard the prayer of His unworthy servant and restored David to his throne. Through the years, until David's ripe old age, the Good Shepherd cared for His sheep. David's body grew feeble but his gratitude for God grew ever stronger. Toward the end of life he composed the magnificent words of Psalm 18:

"I will love You, O Lord, my strength" (verse 1). "He sent from above, He took me; He drew me out of many waters. He delivered me from my strong enemy, from those who hated me, for they were too strong for me. They confronted me in the day of my calamity, but the Lord was my support. . . . He delivered me because He delighted in me" (verses 16-19).

"As for God, His way is perfect; the word of the Lord is proven; He is a shield to all who trust in Him" (verse 30). "You have also given me the shield of Your salvation; Your right hand has held me up, Your gentleness has made me great" (verse 35).

The gentleness of God made David great. It's like that with our children, isn't it? Our gentleness toward them gives them security and confidence to reach their potential, to be all they can be. So it is in Christian living. God's gentle grace gives us the assurance of salvation, giving us the power to grow.

You might feel like a spiritual dwarf, however, intimidated by the eloquence of David's psalms. But really, do we need a fancy vocabulary to impress the Lord?

No, we can just relax and be ourselves with God. He's our friend! We can just open our heart and let it all tumble out.

Jesus said we must become like little children. You know how they are—simple, trusting, affectionate.

Of course, kids don't always set a good example. I think of the little girl who prayed, "Lord, please make Boston the capital of Vermont, because I said so on my test paper." Some things, like the capital of Vermont, might never be changed. Not even through prayer. In our limited wisdom, we don't know what needs altering and what doesn't. So when we pray, shouldn't we trust the results to God? Whether we are asking for healing, or marriage, or anything else—our Father in heaven knows best about when and how to answer the prayers of His children.

Many people ask, How long should I spend praying? The question reminds me of what they asked Abraham Lincoln: "How long should a man's legs be?" You know his answer: "Long enough to reach the ground."

That's how long our prayers should be—long enough to get down to solid ground with God. Some days we need more time in prayer than other days. The point is to invest whatever time it takes to meet the day's needs and deepen our fellowship with the Lord.

Doesn't it make sense to discipline ourselves in setting a regular hour to begin morning prayer? Then we are sure to have all the time we need with God.

Often in prayer I feel great unworthiness nearly overwhelming me. Then I remember God's mercy, and that makes me feel better. Psalm 73 has come to be my favorite when I feel bad about some failure:

"I was senseless and ignorant; I was a brute beast before you. Yet I am always with you; you hold me by my right hand. You guide me with your counsel, and afterward you will take me into glory. . . . My flesh and my heart may fail, but God is the strength of my heart, and my portion forever" (verses 22-26, NIV).

Thank the Lord for His mercy. Even when we fail in our intentions to please Him, He remains with us, loving us and guiding our lives. Doesn't it make you want to serve Him with all your heart?

More of my favorite psalms:

Psalm 16

Psalm 25

Psalm 34

Psalm 40

Psalm 139

Chapter 3

John's Fatal Mistake

Back in the sixties, John Lennon made a fatal mistake. He tried to revolutionize society without reference to Jesus. "Give peace a chance," he preached. Yet an unrelenting restlessness ravaged his own life.

"All you need is love," he sang. Yet he deteriorated into a paranoid hermit who found it hard to show affection to his own child. [1]

"Drugs will set you free," Lennon promised by making his albums a thinly veiled sales pitch for LSD, heroin, and marijuana. Yet chemical addiction enslaved his own body, mind, and soul with bonds he couldn't break.

John Lennon was a loser. He was not what he appeared to be. And millions of his disciples suffered the same psychedelic nightmare. The hippies weren't really happy, you know, despite their flowers and peace marches and all that talk about love.

How could they have peace apart from the Prince of Peace? How could they find love without the Lord of love? And how could they be free while mired in their mind-blowing madness?

When John Lennon and his fellow Beatles first invaded America in 1964, they seemed to have it all. But even in those glory days things were "never that good," recalled

George Harrison in his book appropriately entitled *I, Me, Mine*. "We were like monkeys in a zoo." "Even the best thrill soon got tiring."

Nevertheless, the Beatles' gospel of drugs, sex, and social revolution enraptured the younger generation. In time, though, the big party ended, and the "fabulous four" dissolved in bitter dissension. Lennon became a pale and lonesome invalid. Here's his own pitiful testimony, as reported in *People*:

"I'd lie in bed all day, not talk, not eat, just withdraw. I felt like a hollow temple filled with many spirits, each one passing through me, each inhabiting me for a little time and then leaving, to be replaced by another."

John Lennon was helpless to defend himself against such tormenting demons, without the power of Jesus Christ. In his struggle to divorce himself from drug addiction he had his friends tie him to a chair with only one arm free to hold a cigarette. Roped in that position, he sat for three long days, burning and then freezing, convulsed in agony and begging for release.

Despite the most determined effort of his legendary will, John Lennon could not set himself free. Not even with the help of religion. In the late sixties he and his fellow Beatles had made a pilgrimage to India, there to sit at the feet of the Maharishi Yogi. Nothing Lennon learned from Eastern religion brought him personal power and peace.

Yes, John Lennon did try religion to give peace a chance in his life. But he never gave Jesus Christ a chance. Therein lay his mistake.

Late one December night in 1980, one of Lennon's fans ambushed him and shot him to death. In a sense, though, he had already died years before when he rejected salvation in Jesus for counterfeit fulfillment in Eastern religion and drugs. Lennon's tragic legacy proves the truth of Scripture's warning: "There is a way that seems right to a man but in the end it leads to death" (Proverbs 16:25). [2]

By way of striking contrast to John Lennon's dark life stands the shining example of Paul the apostle. Lennon languished in a dungeon of sin, but Paul was imprisoned for a different reason—faith in Christ. Listen to his triumphant testimony:

"Grace and peace to you from God our Father and the Lord Jesus Christ. I thank my God every time I remember you. In all my prayers for all of you, I always pray with joy because of your partnership in the gospel" (Philippians 1:2-5).

The apostle's heart overflowed with rejoicing amid thoroughly discouraging circumstances. What was his secret of happiness? It was the relationship he had with the Saviour:

"I consider everything a loss compared to the surpassing greatness of knowing Christ Jesus my Lord, for whose sake I have lost all things. I consider them rubbish, that I may gain Christ and be found in him" (Philippians 3:8, 9).

In the love of Jesus Paul discovered "the peace of God, which transcends all understanding" (Philippians 4:7). As a result, he said, "I have learned to be content whatever the circumstances." "I can do everything through him who gives me strength" (verses 11, 13).

It was an experience quite different from the frustrations that he depicted in Romans 7: "For what I do is not the good I want to do; no, the evil I do not want to do—this I keep on doing" (verse 19). Paul knew the difficulty of resisting temptation even as one tried to live a pure life. "For in my inner being I delight in God's law; but I see another law at work in the members of my body, waging war against the law of my mind and making me a prisoner of the law of sin at work within my members. What a wretched man I am! Who will rescue me from this body of death?" (verses 22-24).

Paul's heart was in the right place. In all of Romans 7 we see nothing but wholehearted yearning after goodness, total dedication to pleasing God. Unfortunately, the apostle discovered to his dismay that somehow he was allergic to religion.

Perhaps you suffer an allergy to something you like. Lots of people who love cats, for instance, can't stop sneezing around them. They have to shun their furry friends. Likewise, Paul delighted in God's law, but his flesh was allergic to it: "We know that the law is spiritual, but I am unspiritual, sold as a slave to sin" (verse 14).

Can you relate to such spiritual frustration? Most Christians know such spiritual failures all too well. With appetite, for example, we may find ourselves lamenting, "I can't believe I ate the whole thing!"

Other things trouble us, like resentment. "Who does she think she is!"

Criticism: "Another boring sermon!"

Gossip: "Say, did you hear about . . . ?"

Lust: "I can't believe I just watched that awful movie!"

Greed: "As soon as we get the new stereo, then we'll buy . . ."

Thank God for His forgiveness when we fail—but don't we also want His help in conquering the countless temptations that come our way every day? Must we remain the helpless slaves of sin?

In Jesus Christ we find power to transform our lives. The apostle Paul discovered the secret he described in Romans 6:14: "For sin shall not be your master, because you are not under law, but under grace."

That is good news indeed—slavery to sin ends when we learn to live "not under law, but under grace." But just what does this mean? Let's look at the life of Paul and find out.

In his younger days he attempted to please God by measuring up to the law. But after his encounter with Christ, Paul came to see that his quest to fulfill the law's requirements only intensified his sin problem.

Of course, the law itself had nothing wrong with it. It is from God Himself. We need it to tell us right from wrong. The apostle said, "I would not have known what sin was except through the law. For I would not have known what it was to covet if the law had not said, 'Do not covet'" (Romans 7:7).

Unfortunately, something happened inside him when the law pointed out his guilt: "Sin, taking opportunity through the commandment, produced in me coveting of every kind; for apart from the Law sin is dead" (verse 8, NASB). Sinful human nature takes advantage of the commandment "Do not covet," to produce the very behavior forbidden. And this happens despite earnest commitment to obey God's holy law. Paul even said that sin has no power apart from the law. How could this be?

The law makes us feel guilty, which only worsens our spiritual situation. Guilt breeds discouragement, and that paralyzes us from resisting additional attacks of temptation. Finding ourselves deeper in sin than ever, we're ready to be rescued from religion—all because we feel condemned by the law.

Utterly despondent, Paul might have figured, "What's the use, anyway?" That would have made him feel worse off than ever. Paralyzed by depression and lured by sin, he would be headed for spiritual failure.

But the law itself was not at fault for his failure. As he forcefully pointed out, God's Ten Commandments are "holy, righteous and good" (verse 12). They tell us right from wrong. Yet in doing so, they expose our sinfulness so efficiently and vigorously that we become hopeless and desperate.

It's a vicious cycle. The law condemns our guilt and leaves us discouraged, driving us deeper and deeper into sin. And the deeper we fall into sin, the more the law condemns us. No wonder the Bible concludes that "the power of sin is the law" (1 Corinthians 15:56).

So for us to live under the law as a way of salvation will yield only failure and despair. How nice it would be to flee to the saving arms of Jesus. And such an escape is possible! We can be forgiven fully and freely through the Lord Jesus Christ.

Sinners can find acceptance with God because our Saviour's life and death fulfilled the law's requirements on our behalf. This is the good news of the gospel. God accepts us as perfect in Christ, just as if we never had done anything wrong—just as if we had always done everything right! (see Ephesians 1:6, 7 and Colossians 2:9, 10).

Does saving grace, then, release us from spiritual responsibility? Are we free to "do our own thing," as John Lennon did? Paul tells us in no uncertain terms: "Do we, then, nullify the law by this faith? Not at all! Rather, we uphold the law" (Romans 3:31).

The Bible says that we "died to the law through the body of Christ . . . that we might bear fruit to God" (Romans 7:4). This is victory over sin, contrasting with the "fruit for death" we bore in the old life.

Living under grace provides power to obey God. According to the apostle Paul, "We have been released from the law so that we serve in the new way of the Spirit, and not in the old way of the written code" (verse 6). The word *serve* in Paul's day literally meant "to slave." You wouldn't expect a slave to run around town doing as he pleased. He must obey his master's will. So with the Christian—we serve Jesus. We live according to His will, not ours.

Legalism is a struggle with the responsibility of measuring up to God's standards. But Paul discovered the freedom to serve the Lord without fretting about his own character shortcomings. Such an atmosphere of acceptance and assurance sparked a spiritual growth spurt. Sin lost its dominion, and he bore the fruit of love for God.

Love for God—what does it actually mean? Is it warm feelings in our hearts when we worship? It is far more than that: "For this is the love of God, that we keep His commandments. And His commandments are not burdensome" (1 John 5:3, NKJV).

Obedience isn't a burden when we are saved by grace. If we looked to the law to earn our salvation through our works, we would feel crushed under the task of satisfying its endless demands. But with God's free gift of salvation, our hearts respond in gratitude and love for Him—and we then honor those same Ten Commandments which used to seem so oppressive.

Of course, we still fall short of God's glorious ideal, but no sincere believer need worry. "Therefore, there is now no condemnation for those who are in Christ Jesus" (Romans 8:1).

Temptations remain, of course. Everyone in the present world has a fallen nature, suffering from sinful predispositions of one kind or another. Some may be especially susceptible to alcoholism, others to an uncontrolled appetite, still others to violence and abuse. Women appear more prone to become depressed. Men seem to struggle more with physical lust. We all battle problems.

Living under grace, however, provides the believer with God's power to overcome. Therefore, nobody can excuse himself for indulging in sin, no matter what the individual predisposition. Thank God, He also offers mercy when we fail to fulfill our potential.

The Christian life requires wrestling with reality. As long as we remain on earth our sinful flesh will harass us with temptation: "For the flesh lusts against the Spirit, and the Spirit against the flesh; and these are contrary to one another, so that you do not do the things that you wish" (Galatians 5:17, NKJV).

All Christians experience the battle between two opposing forces—the old nature of the flesh and the new nature of the Spirit. We may find ourselves haunted by habits formed in years past. Their attractions and feelings certainly annoy us, but they don't amount to sin as long as we refuse to yield to them.

Here's a delightfully simple formula for successful Christian living: "But put on the Lord Jesus Christ, and make no provision for the flesh, to fulfill its lusts" (Romans 13:14, NKJV).

Notice the first step Paul outlines—we clothe ourselves with Jesus, trusting in His righteousness instead of our own works. And we deepen our relationship with Jesus by studying His Word, seeking to know Him. Evidently we must take our personal prayer life seriously, disciplining ourselves in our busy schedules to spend time alone every day with God.

Now for the second part of that success formula: "Make no provision for the flesh, to fulfill its lusts." That means we refuse to pamper our sinful nature, going the second mile to escape temptation wherever possible. We may find it necessary to drastically change our environment to avoid the lure of the old life. Only in this way can we prevent the lusts of the flesh—the drives of our imperfect nature and bodies—from reclaiming our souls.

Legalism can also drag us down again to sin, so let's remember the first part of Paul's success formula: clothing ourselves in the righteousness of Jesus. As long as we keep living under grace, guilt gives way to peace and power.

Now back to the tragic life of John Lennon and the parallels we find with the apostle Paul. Both moved the world—one helped turn it upside down, the other rightside up. Both struggled with the flesh—one died the slave of psychedelic sin, the other found victory in Jesus. Both died prematurely—and both will be resurrected to face their individual reward: "Do not be amazed at this, for a time is coming when all who are in their graves will hear his [Christ's] voice and come out—those who have done good will rise to live, and those who have done evil will rise to be condemned" (John 5:28, 29).

(Let's not get confused here. Our good works cannot earn us a ticket to heaven, but they do reveal whether we have entrusted ourselves to the Lord Jesus.)

John Lennon had no assurance for eternity. He worried about what would happen when he died, and he expressed horror at the thought of cremation. In spite of that fear, his widow ignored the instructions in his will for a traditional funeral and burial. The evening after Lennon died, a security agent entered his apartment building carrying a package about a foot high, disguised by colorful holiday wrappings. "What's that?" someone asked. "That," replied the man, "was the greatest rock musician in the world."

It was indeed "a hard day's night" for John Lennon, not to mention what the future may hold for him. But the apostle Paul, as a sincere believer in Jesus, had no reason to fear for eternity. Just before his death he testified,

"I have fought the good fight, I have finished the race, I have kept the faith. Now there is in store for me the crown of righteousness, which the Lord, the righteous Judge, will award to me on that day—and not only to me, but also to all who have longed for his appearing" (2 Timothy 4:7, 8).

The choice is yours. That of John Lennon or the apostle Paul—whose example will you follow?

If you want more:
John 15:4-8
Romans 8
Romans 15:13
Philippians 4
Hebrews 8:10-12

---

[1] I have extracted biographical information about Lennon from the best-selling biography by Albert Goldman, *The Lives of John Lennon*.

[2] All texts in this chapter are from the New International Version.

Chapter 4

Pam's Tortured Conscience

Twelve years ago Pam gave her heart to Jesus. As she rejoiced in her new salvation, power over sin surged into her life. She imagined that within a few weeks she could be perfect—just like Jesus—through faith in His indwelling strength.

Somehow that didn't happen, and guilt mingled with doubt began gnawing at her conscience: "Since I'm not anywhere near perfect yet, I wonder if I'm worthy of heaven. . . . Suppose I'm not even saved anymore!"

Pam confided her confusion to a friend, who came up with some quick advice: "You're trying to do it all by yourself, silly! Just let go, and let Jesus live His perfect life in you."

But Pam remained perplexed. "How do I do that?"

"You missed the point—He does it!"

"But He won't do it without me. I must have some part to do."

"Well, you know, just surrender your will to Jesus every morning and nurture that relationship with Him. Then when temptation comes, Christ will naturally live out His victory within you—as long as you don't resist."

That sounded sensible, but she had already been surrendering her life to Jesus in sincere prayer every day. Now she increased her devotional time, studying the character of Christ with the intensity of a college senior prepping for a final exam.

Still she found no spiritual satisfaction. In fact, her sense of guilt even worsened. You see, the more she learned about Jesus, the more aware she became of her own unlikeness to the Lord. That left her with deeper hopelessness than ever. Often she rose from her knees in greater despair than when she began praying.

Pam also got discouraged when she compared herself with women in her prayer group who seemed to enjoy a closer relationship with Jesus than she did. They reveled in being filled by the Holy Spirit and reported all kinds of star-spangled answers to prayer. Poor Pam couldn't recall any of her prayers being answered. Nothing major, anyway.

Intimidated by those super-saints, she consoled herself by contrasting her sober lifestyle with church members who apparently lacked commitment. Those who didn't join prayer groups, didn't have daily devotions, or didn't send their kids to Christian schools.

Although Pam hated herself for indulging in such a "holier than thou" attitude, she couldn't make herself stop. Self-righteousness provided the only refuge from a torturing conscience.

Her friends considered her one of the most helpful and humble Christians they knew. She wasn't all that happy, they could tell, but her pious convictions impressed them. Even so, guilt, like a nagging toothache, hounded her constantly. Pam hated to admit it, yet it was true just the same: she had actually been happier before becoming a Christian!

Before long she secretly resented religion for ruining her life (which made her feel all the more guilty). Why go on trying to please God? What was the use?

Finally she decided to discuss her frustrations with her pastor. There in the church office she opened the conversation. "I've always admired you, Pastor. You seem to know the whole Bible backward and forward. I wish I knew the Lord as you do."

"And I admire many of your qualities too, Pam," he responded. "But both of us have a serious problem. The apostle Paul exposes it in Romans 3. Notice verses 22 and 23: 'There is no difference, for all have sinned and fall short of the glory of God.'

"You see, all of us fall short of perfection. So there is no difference, no distinction—none are better or worse than others in the church. We all deserve damnation."

She looked startled as he continued.

"Really, none of us are any more worthy than the most desperate criminal cringing on death row. We don't even deserve the polluted air we breathe. When you hold up my life, or your life—or anyone's life—comparing it to Christ's character, we all come up short. Evidently there's no ground for comparisons. We're all equally unworthy."

Pam observed with a rueful smile, "In other words, I'm not OK—but at least you're not OK either! That doesn't leave us with much hope, does it?"

"Well, we can be thankful the story doesn't end there. Listen to this good news: 'But God, who is rich in mercy, because of His great love with which He loved us, even when we were dead in trespasses, made us alive together with Christ (by grace you have been saved)' (Ephesians 2:4, 5).

"Do you see what has happened now? We are alive together in the Lord Jesus Christ. Before, we were doomed together. But now in Jesus we are redeemed together. So we're equal again."

Pam perked up as the pastor added,"Let me tell you about Lisa, a new believer in a church I used to serve. She compared herself with older Christians and got discouraged. They seemed to have a better prayer vocabulary than she did. Or they didn't appear bothered with the doubts and struggles she faced. Soon Lisa developed a spiritual inferiority complex.

"She would have been shocked to realize that many of the older Christians envied her—the same ones she put on a pedestal. Her fresh faith and eager enthusiasm for the Lord made them nervous. They felt threatened by her. Seeking to build themselves up, they put her down, finding in her young spiritual life things to criticize. Feeling condemned, Lisa finally got so depressed she almost left the church."

"I know how that feels," Pam interjected. "I've been on the verge of giving up too."

"That's tragic! How few of us really know the gospel. The gospel that makes us all equal—equally lost without Jesus, equally saved in Christ. Whatever our level of Christian growth, all of us share the same perfect record of Jesus Christ. We must all approach God through His mercy, not on the basis of our character development. Our hope, you see, is never in our spiritual attainments, but in Christ's sacrifice for us on the cross. And our assurance of salvation is not our feeble love for God, but His great love for us in Christ.

"Our foolish comparisons!" the pastor continued, shaking his head. "They always create barriers of inferiority, hypocrisy, intolerance—barriers that Jesus tore down at the cross. There is no difference now between believers. We are either saved or lost—no second-class Christians. And no super-saints who stand more acceptable before God than the poorest struggling believer."

Pam looked excited. "This is such a wonderful concept that it's hard to get hold of. Let me see if I can put it in my own words. When I accept Jesus as my Saviour, God considers me as perfect as He is—even though I'm very much imperfect. Is that it? And since you have accepted Jesus, you're counted just that perfect too. We all share Christ's perfection—there's no difference now! That means that I don't have to feel intimidated again by anyone!

"Well," she concluded, "I guess I don't have to prove myself to other Christians. Not even to God! He loves and accepts me completely in Jesus."

"Amen!" the pastor concurred. "Day by day, Pam, just cast yourself upon God's mercy and obey His will. When you fall, confess your sin and ask for His help next time around. As you keep committing your life to Him, He will keep counting you perfect in Jesus. Keep resting in His love, and He will quietly develop in you a character that will honor Him and make you a great blessing in this world."

All that week she thought over what she had learned from the pastor. It all made sense. For the first time in years, rays of hope and peace began brightening her life.

Next weekend at church the pastor shared lessons from the life of Abraham. Called in Scripture the father of the faithful, the ancient patriarch's original name was Abram, and his wife's name was Sarai. They lived in the city of Ur, within the present Persian Gulf region of Iraq. God called them out of their homeland with the promise to make them the parents of a great nation.

Abram and Sarai accepted the Lord's call by faith, wandering obediently from place to place before finally settling in the area we know as Israel. Finally the time came for God to fulfill His promise. That was the night the Lord summoned Abram outside his tent and urged him to look up at the desert sky. "See the stars? So shall the number of your descendants be," God declared.

Quite a promise indeed, especially for an elderly couple with no children of their own. Then God announced another surprise. He invited them immediately to consider themselves the parents of a great nation and even changed their names to reflect their parenthood. "No longer shall your name be called Abram, but your name shall be Abraham; for I have made you a father of many nations" (Genesis 17:5). Sarai's name God altered to Sarah, which meant "mother of many nations."

It took quite some faith for Abraham and Sarah to accept their new names. How could a man 100 years old and his childless wife of 90 consider themselves already the parents of many nations? Humanly speaking, the idea was foolish. So ridiculous that Abraham "fell on his face and laughed" right there in the presence of God.

Eventually Abraham and Sarah grasped God's promise, and He counted their faith as righteousness. Remember that God had already declared them to be parents—something they were not, something they were completely unworthy of considering themselves to be. But by faith they welcomed their new names anyway.

Through the experience of Abraham and Sarah we learn about the faith by which we are saved. We must accept God's declaration of something we are not—God "justifies [forgives] the ungodly," according to Romans 4:5. When we repent and believe, the Lord counts us perfect through the blood of Christ—even though we are totally unworthy.

God does not leave us helplessly trapped in failure, however. Alcoholics become sober through God's grace. Adulterers become trustworthy spouses. We forgive others as God has forgiven us.

Faith also transformed the lives of Abraham and Sarah. She gave birth to Isaac, the miracle child of promise. And just as faith worked miracles for Abraham and Sarah, faith in Christ will bring about the miracle of transformed lives today.

No, salvation by grace doesn't give us permission to fool around with sin. God offers all the power we need to keep from yielding to temptation. But let's be careful here. Victory over sin never becomes the basis of our salvation. The miracle of a changed life never becomes our ticket to heaven.

Remember Abraham's miracle child Isaac. As the young fellow matured and bore children of his own, did Abraham become more worthy to bear the title "father of many nations"? No, from beginning to end it was God's mercy alone—not that miracle in Abraham's life—that qualified him for acceptance with Him. Likewise with us. Sincere faith will bring victories over sin, but such miracles never become the basis of whether God can accept us. Only through the blood of Christ are we ever worthy of heaven.

Well, that was quite a sermon for Pam. Learning about Abraham really helped her understand the good news of salvation. Questions lingered, of course, so the following week she visited the church office again.

"You've helped me a lot, Pastor, but I'm still perplexed. What about the Holy Spirit? How can the Holy Spirit live in my heart unless I first achieve holiness myself?"

"The Spirit lives within us because God has already made us His children through Jesus—not because we are worthy," her minister explained. "Remember Abraham. The Holy Spirit gave him power to become a father, but that was only after God had already accepted him as the father of many nations."

"But what if I momentarily resist the Holy Spirit and yield to temptation? Like if I get mad at the kids. Am I lost at that moment?"

"No, thank God. Abraham failed too from time to time—he even lied about being married to Sarah. Yet the Bible says he did not waver from his faithfulness. He wobbled, but he didn't waver! It's the general trend of our lives, not some occasional good deed or misdeed, that shows whether we are genuine Christians.

"You know, Pam, along the gospel freeway lie two opposite ditches, equally treacherous. Off to the left you have the ditch of presumption—people thinking they are saved while refusing to surrender themselves to Christ. To them, forsaking their sinful ways is something optional —nice but not necessary. They overlook that faith in Christ involves a covenant with Him, an agreement similar to the marriage commitment.

"Since you are conscientious, Pam, your big battle isn't with presumption. Your tendency is to fall into the opposite ditch, legalism—basing your salvation on your spiritual accomplishments rather than rejoicing in what Jesus has already done as your Saviour. You've got to guard against that and keep trusting in the blood of Jesus."

"But Pastor, I want so much to overcome every sin!"

"The devil knows that, and all these years he's been taking advantage of your sincerity. It seems incredible, but it's true just the same—many earnest Christians actually compete against Christ. Seeking to equal His perfect character, they fail to find refuge in Him as their substitute. Yes, they go to Him for strength, but they don't trust His blood to cover their shortcomings. Because of such legalism they never find rest."

"You're right. I've been miserable all these years."

"Pam, you might have been confusing what the Bible calls the 'fruit' of the gospel—a changed life—with the gospel itself. The gospel, you see, is the life, death, and resurrection of Christ. The fruit of the gospel is a transformed life because of the indwelling Christ. Do you see the difference?" [1]

"I certainly do. I guess I've been making my pattern of Christian growth the basis of my salvation—rather than finding my security in the blood of Jesus."

"You've got it. Christian living offers all kinds of possibilities, but my faith must remain rooted in God's forgiveness. I could memorize 10 books of the Bible during the next year, perhaps the entire New Testament. But if I fall short of that goal, am I lost? It might be possible for me to win my whole neighborhood to Christ this coming year. But suppose I fail—am I lost? It's possible for me to be such a good father that I run circles around Bill Cosby. But am I lost if I simply love my children and show them Jesus?"

"Spiritual security is wonderful, Pastor. But how far does it go? Once I'm saved, is it impossible for me to become lost?"

"Well, think of a married couple. Nobody in the world can rob them of their relationship, but they can forfeit it themselves by their own free choice. The national divorce rate tragically attests that there's no such thing as once married, always married. We Christians likewise must preserve our relationship with Christ throughout life. God keeps us in His grace, but only as we continue yielding ourselves to Him. If we return to our old lifestyle, we squander our salvation." [2]

"Well," she responded, "since it is possible to become lost again, at what point would we forfeit our salvation?"

"Suppose a husband and wife have a little argument. They might say things that don't reflect the love they really do cherish for each other. Later they feel ashamed and deeply sorry. So they confess to each other and make up. Now tell me. After they have cleared the air with their confession, must they go down to the county courthouse and get married again?"

"Certainly not," she answered, laughing at the absurdity of the suggestion.

"Now, if they refused to admit their guilt and stubbornly denied their sinfulness, that marriage would ultimately be lost. Any problem, even something small, can eventually split apart a relationship unless it is confessed and confronted. So in the Christian life. We must confess specific sin—nip it in the bud before it becomes a cherished sin, something more important to us than Jesus. Otherwise, at that point we would indeed lose our salvation. Thank God, though, we don't have to live in the dungeon of spiritual insecurity. Having entrusted ourselves to Jesus we can know we are saved."

"But what happens when I don't feel saved?"

"Feelings often fool us, Pam. People with terminal cancer often feel fine, unaware of their fatal condition. On the other hand, we might feel awful when really nothing is wrong.

"Spiritually, too, feelings often fail to tell the truth. We might have great confidence about heaven even while lost outside of Christ. And we might struggle with guilt when everything is fine with our relationship with our Lord."

"I think I'm understanding that now, Pastor. But there's something else that really bothers me. Often I feel impatient or resentful, and I ask the Lord to take those desires to sin away. But I still have those cravings—even when I spend a lot of time with Jesus."

"Pam, you could spend the whole day praying, and still the fact remains that you have a sinful nature that produces those cravings."

"But doesn't the Bible say we'll get a new heart?"

"That means a new attitude, a new willingness to resist temptation and follow Jesus. Cravings of the flesh remain to tempt us. Listen to this from the book of James: 'Each one is tempted when he is drawn away by his own desires and enticed' [James 1:14]. So we all have desires for sin that conflict with our commitment. The important thing is that we don't yield to those urges."

"But I wish God would take all those sinful cravings away!"

"That won't happen until Jesus comes, when He will change our vile bodies into ones like His glorious body. Till then, the Spirit and the flesh battle it out, and it's up to us to make the right choices."

"Can't I just let go and let Jesus fight my battles?"

"The Bible says we must fight the good fight of faith and 'run with endurance the race that is set before us, looking unto Jesus' [Hebrews 12:1, 2]. God's Word has a lot to say about effort, Pam. It takes effort to get up in the morning to spend time with Jesus. It takes effort when temptation comes to turn to God for help. God gives strength, but we must trust Him for it. That's not always easy."

"Well, Pastor, all this is wonderful! I sure hope I remember everything so I don't lose my peace with God."

"Pam, peace with God isn't an emotion that comes and goes. It's a state of legal innocence that is ours through the gospel. Whether or not we feel peace, we can know that we have it with God through our Lord Jesus Christ [Romans 5:1]. Pleasant feelings are nice, but they're not necessary to be saved—a surrendered heart entrusted to Christ is what counts."

Pam looked relieved as she departed the pastor's office. She left behind her all her years of insecurity and uncertainty, of being tortured by her conscience. Now her life is a pageant of rejoicing in Jesus.

How about you? Why not give yourself a spiritual checkup? Have you repented of your sins and accepted Jesus as your Saviour and Lord? If so, then, thank God, your sins are forgiven. When God looks down from heaven He smiles at you and says, "This is Joe, my beloved son, in whom I am well pleased."

"Oh no, Lord," you may protest, "You can't be happy with me—I'm still struggling with problems. After I conquer them, I can consider myself worthy to be Your child."

God responds, "I've got the power to help you overcome your problems. But even now you are 'accepted in the Beloved,' 'you are complete in Him' (Ephesians 1:6;

Colossians 2:10). Not because you are worthy but because you have accepted the life of My Son."

"God has given us eternal life, and this life is in His Son. He who has the Son has life; he who does not have the Son of God does not have life. These things have I written to you who believe in the name of the Son of God, that you may know that you have eternal life" (1 John 5:11-13).

If you want more:
Romans 3:20-31
Romans 8:1-4
Colossians 1:21-23
Ephesians 2:8-10

---

[1] Colossians 1:4-6 clearly distinguishes between the "word of the truth of the gospel" and the "fruit" of the gospel, a victorious life.

[2] Consider the parable Jesus told in Matthew 18 about the unjust servant. His master had set him free from a huge debt, yet the ungrateful man refused to pass along that forgiveness. He went out and hunted down someone who owed him a pittance, threatening the poor debtor. The unforgiving servant had his own forgiveness canceled. Other texts that warn against forfeiting salvation are Matthew 24:13, Colossians 1:22, 23, and 1 Corinthians 9:27.

Chapter 5

Judy Finds Prince Charming

Meet Greg. He's a 29-year-old TV producer who likes Hollywood women but doesn't have time to "service" a long-term commitment. So he and his special girlfriend spend several nights a week together enjoying a "low-maintenance, low-stress" romance.

"I'm into lite relationships," Greg explains. "Lite relationships, just like lite beer—all the taste but half the calories. All the relationship but half the baggage."

And how does his girlfriend react to such an arrangement? "It's not an issue," Greg insists. "How can I make a commitment now to love someone in the year 2010?"

Well, Greg has lots of allies among his fellow bachelors. Men love women—but why don't more men want to love them forever?

The *Los Angeles Times Magazine* scouted the singles' scene in southern California in a recent article entitled "Lite Romance." Their staff writer interviewed women who had been searching for Prince Charming (or some reasonable substitute).

Karen, a 32-year-old floral designer in Santa Ana, pondered the question "What's the matter with men?" Her reply: "They fill your head with 'Oh, let's get married and have children.' And they are hot and heavy for a week or a month. Then they disappear."

Kelly, an executive secretary in west LA, also lamented her failed friendships with men. "You give so much of yourself, and then they freak out."

Sally, who supports herself by reviewing movie scripts, confessed to similar frustration as she talked with the *Times*. "I was never eager to get married when I was younger," she said. "But now I'm 36, and I haven't had a boyfriend in three years."

It's not that she is homely or shy or that she harbors unreasonable expectations. "I'm not asking that he look like Don Johnson. But I am asking that his socks match." Sally proceeded to detail her tribulations. "I dress up for a party and not a single man speaks to me. And the ones I speak to—they walk away."

Her friends console her, suggesting that her good looks intimidate men. But if that's true, she asks, "How come every box boy in town isn't the slightest bit intimidated? Or tow truck drivers? They are forever asking me for dates."

She likes men and always has, but she can't figure them out. Weary of all the good-time Charlies who have paraded through her life, she's becoming desperate in her loneliness. And there's no solution in sight.

Betsy, a 43-year-old counselor in the San Fernando Valley, shares Sally's perplexities. "Where are all the good ones? All the men our age are either married or sleeping under bridges."

It's just about that bad, according to a recent Harvard-Yale study quoted by *Newsweek*. The survey found that a college-educated White woman still single at age 30 has only a 20 percent prospect of marrying. By the time she reaches the ripe old age of 35, her chances drop to 5 percent. For a 40-year-old woman, the Harvard-Yale survey rated the odds of getting married as "minuscule"—2.6 percent.

To put it bluntly, if you are single and over 40, your chances of landing Prince Charming are so slim that you are more likely to be killed by a terrorist!

Thanks a lot! Other social studies dispute the Harvard-Yale findings and declare that the single woman's prospects aren't nearly so pitiful. After all, the eligible male human being isn't on the endangered species list. Not yet, anyway. But the experts agree that available men are far too scarce for the millions of lonely women looking for life companions.

Many single men hear these things and scratch their heads. They wonder why they can't locate the woman of their choice among their social contacts. Steve, a good-natured yuppie-type guy, expressed frustration in finding someone whose expectations he could satisfy. "It's no fun having a woman always tell you what's wrong with you. The girls I date seem to be saying, 'I'm OK, but you had better be perfect.'"

Evidently some decent men are willing and waiting to walk up the aisle. There must be ways to find them, wherever they are hiding. In a few moments we'll discover how to locate Prince Charming, but first let's ask ourselves, Why the shortage of marriage-minded men?

To begin with, more women inhabit our world than men for them to match up with. A male's shorter life expectancy further drains off the pool of potential husbands. But the unhappy reality of overpopulation can't bear all the blame. Several other factors, such as the homosexuality epidemic, tend to torpedo the love boat. Nobody knows the exact facts, but experts report a higher proportion of gay males than females. One observer estimates that three times as many men are committed to the homosexual lifestyle. With so many single men dating themselves, the lineup of available bachelors has thinned out even more.

Have you ever been attracted to a single guy, only to find out that he's gay? Many have suffered such heartbreak. Every gay relationship between men robs two women of life companions.

Another problem single woman have is society's approval of good-time Charlie. Back in the 1950s we frowned upon bachelors who withheld themselves from a wife and family. But by the 1970s staying single became the "macho" alternative. Now irresponsible bachelors can consider themselves respectable citizens. When they finally get ready to settle down—whether that nesting instinct comes at age 25 or 45—women will be waiting with open arms.

Men seem to have it made. As one contented bachelor put it: "Women are under the big-time crunch. They don't have forever, the way a man does."

So much for equal-opportunity dating. There ought to be a law, it seems, to protect the rights of single women. But what good would it do? You can't legislate love!

Up to this point every cause of their dating misfortunes lies beyond the control of single women. But they can largely blame themselves for what may be the major cause of the crisis—female consent to the sexual revolution.

Things may be changing now. After a quarter century of anything goes, the sexual revolution seems to be running out of steam somewhat. Is God's way the only way after all? Is it true that Father knows best?

I'm not preaching here—just asking questions. But enough about the problem before we all get depressed. Let's search for a solution.

Now I would like to tell you about someone who finally found Prince Charming—Judy, 36 years old, who works for a Los Angeles law firm. You wouldn't call her beautiful, but she's reasonably attractive. Before she added 15 stubborn pounds to her figure, she often noticed men at restaurants looking her over and would wink at them. That was fun.

Judy enjoyed those encounters, all right, but they led nowhere. She pressed onward in her search for that special man. Each morning she sped to work in a red Mustang sporting that celebrated bumper sticker "Happiness Is Being Single." Nonsense as far as Judy was concerned, but it pays to advertise. At least that's what she hoped.

Then came the day that the Harvard-Yale study on single women hit the news wires (the one you read about a few moments ago). That same afternoon she came home from work to find her phone ringing.

Prince Charming? No, it was Mother.

"Judy," she implored, "you've got to get out of the house and meet someone. Now!"

"OK, Mom, as soon as I have a bite of supper, if you don't mind. But where do I go?"

That was the big question—where to go to find a life companion. Judy intensified her quest. She became quite creative, even taking a cruise to Hawaii. Unfortunately, her plans for romance sank before the love boat docked.

Then she scouted the singles' bars once or twice, but found nobody there. Nobody except the ever-present good-time Charlies with their unbuttoned shirts, gold jewelry, and herpes. Maybe even AIDS.

The thought made her shiver. No use sacrificing her life on the altar of their fickle lust.

Men around the office seemed nice, in a shallow sort of way. Some of them even invited her to lunch now and then, but it turned out they wanted nothing more than a quick frolic at the motel. A time or two Judy succumbed to them, only to find herself abandoned when they vanished to exploit other lonely victims.

"Good riddance, you jerk!" she sobbed between clenched teeth as they skipped out of her life. She wished she could have them arrested and thrown into jail for their arrogance and selfishness.

The most desirable men around the office were already married. *Just my luck,* she thought. Several of them made passes at her anyway. One even invited her for a weekend in Las Vegas.

Some of her friends went to bed with other women's husbands. In fact, 15 to 20 percent of women over 35 have affairs with married men, according to a San Diego State University sociologist. But Judy wanted nothing to do with breaking up a marriage and stealing some little girl's daddy.

No, she decided to stick with single men, for better or for worse. But with her childbearing years slipping by, she found herself desperate with the desire to have a family. Although she tried to hide her feelings, the men who dated her sensed her eagerness to take them to the altar. It scared them away.

The same sad cycle repeated itself constantly. Whenever Judy began liking someone, he dumped her so quickly she hardly knew it was happening again. During a decade of desperate scheming, she never managed to land a man she wanted. She never found someone who would care about her feelings and shelter her from a cold, cruel world.

Finally, just when all hope seemed gone, something wonderful happened. Jack, one of the attorneys at the office, fell in love with her. At last a real relationship to light up her life! Here was a warm and willing heart to melt away her loneliness.

Things started looking pretty promising. Judy even dropped into the bridal shop at the mall and started fantasizing about the wedding. Then Suzy, the new receptionist, arrived on the scene.

Ten years younger, she resembled Cybill Shepherd. To call her cute would be an understatement. You guessed it. She set her sights on Jack (as if he hadn't already been dazzled by her). Within three months they were married.

The day of the wedding dawned sunny and bright, but it was the darkest of Judy's life. That afternoon she drove past the red brick church with its flowers and bridesmaids and hundreds of smiling faces. She stomped on the gas pedal and headed for the bar to quench her pain.

Despite several stiff drinks, she couldn't sleep that night. Not with the man she loved going off to Hawaii for a honeymoon in someone else's arms.

Suicide now became an increasing temptation. Maybe Jack would attend her funeral. If she couldn't get him to the altar, at least he might visit her casket.

After two weeks in paradise, Suzy and Jack came back with suntans and smiles. Judy managed a cheerful facade for them at the office. "I'm just fine, and how are you?"

A big lie, but Judy feared she might lose her job if she dumped her emotional burdens on everybody. As long as she was still alive she had to work. Besides, she would never give Suzy the satisfaction of knowing how much she hurt. Not even if it killed her to keep quiet.

Then one weekend morning, in the depths of her despair, she finally met someone who loved her for herself and gave her comfort and hope for the future. She was lying in bed, still groggy from her nightly dose of Valium as she reached for the small black television remote control. On flashed the screen. Idly flipping through the stations, she passed Popeye and the Flintstones.

Then one telecast caught her attention. A beaming young woman was telling how peace and purpose had entered her life. It seemed that she had met a man who truly loved her and filled her lonely heart with joy.

That new friend was Jesus.

Watching in wonder, Judy saw the delight on that young woman's face and thought, *Religion hasn't done anything much for me so far, but this seems different. Maybe I can reach out to Jesus, too. Nobody else cares about me.*

As she pondered the possibilities of a new life she found herself making the big decision. "Since Jesus wants me, He can have me. Every broken part of my heart. I'm asking Him to be my best friend, to lead me into His special plan for my life."

Well, that was it. Judy found the one the Bible calls the "Prince of Peace"—the one who really understands her and loves her just as she is. The one who comforts her heart through lonely nights and helps her all day long. The only one who never lets her down.

Judy began reading the Bible so she could learn more about her new Friend. To her surprise, she discovered that Jesus could identify with her emotional isolation. Our Lord lived among us as a lonely man, at odds with the establishment of His time. In those quaint words of Scripture, "I have trodden the winepress alone; and of the people there was none with me" (Isaiah 53:3, KJV).

Yes, Jesus was lonely here on earth. He was single too, just like Judy. Not because He wouldn't have wanted to get married—He loved the children who crowded onto His lap and no doubt hungered to have His own family. But He was scheduled to die in His mid-30s as the Saviour of the world.

Besides, He had to travel around, often sleeping out-doors under the olive trees outside Jerusalem. There was no way He could have supported a wife under such circumstances.

So Jesus walked the dusty roads of Palestine as a lonesome wanderer. Never was His emotional distress more apparent than the night before He died. A special kind of loneliness overwhelmed Him there in the moonlit Garden of Gethsemane. (We will look at that further in our next chapter.)

Meanwhile, back to Judy. How did her new life in Jesus affect her relationships with other men? Well, something unexpected is happening. She notices a change in the way they treat her. They seem to sense her new self-esteem, the way she feels good about herself. Her blossoming self-confidence makes her seem independent and mysteriously elusive.

Now Judy has to laugh to herself about that. Who would have ever thought that religion would make her more attractive to men! In a wholesome sort of way, you know. Now she's nobody's plaything anymore, and people respect that.

The men around Judy haven't quite figured her out. She doesn't beg for their interest anymore. She enjoys their attention, certainly, but it's not a matter of life and death as it used to be.

Sometimes Judy does get lonely again. That ugly feeling of emptiness begins to slither back into her life. Then she turns to her new Friend—and He's always there. He's there within the pages of His Word. And through prayer she can talk with Him anytime, and whenever she does, she feels much better.

Judy has joined a Bible study fellowship. Several of the most decent fellows she ever met attend the group. Although more women than men show up, she doesn't feel threatened. Other women aren't her rivals anymore—they are her sisters in Christ. She knows God has a plan just for her, and nobody—*nobody*—can take it away from her. Not Suzy or Jack or anybody else.

If God's plans include wedding bells someday, that would be wonderful. The Lord will work that out whenever He knows she and her fiancé-to-be are ready. All Judy needs to do is to keep her relationship with Jesus as her first priority in life, and all will be well.

A Christian husband would be nice indeed. Yet even now Judy knows she's already much happier than most married women ever will be. At least she's certainly happier than Suzy and Jack have been lately—that she can definitely tell.

Yet Judy wants nothing but the best for those who hurt her most. She prays for the couple and even invited them to visit her Bible study fellowship. And they promised to come!

Jesus has relieved Judy's resentment and healed her wounded heart. Her new life overflows with love and joy and peace. One day soon He will return to earth to take her away, off to an eternal mansion in the paradise that He has prepared for her. She can hardly wait.

Meanwhile, whenever anyone asks her how she's doing, she smiles and says, "I'm just fine—and how are you?" The same answer she's always had. But now she means it. Now it's real.

Would you like to know Judy's Prince? He loves you, too. All these years He's been yearning for your friendship. Nothing else will satisfy your heart. Or His.

If you want more:
Matthew 11:28-30
Philippians 3:7-12
Revelation 3:19, 20

Chapter 6

Mark's New Father

Mark hid behind the neighbor's house as his father's truck roared past. He and his brother were running away from home with their mother. If his father caught them, it would be too bad.

Their narrow escape was not the first time that his mother had taken the boys and vanished. And unfortunately, it wouldn't be the last. Two weeks later the few dollars they had ran out, and Mark's mother had no choice but to return home with her sons.

Home sweet home it wasn't. The emotional abuse became so intense that Mark's brother suffered a nervous breakdown. After that, several Christian neighbors pooled their resources and helped the family escape for good, never to return. The damage was done, however. Both boys suffered lasting emotional scars.

It wasn't that their father drank or did drugs or gambled. Nor did he fly off the handle and lose control of himself. A decent, disciplined man who took a real interest in his sons, he even spent time to teach them every day about God.

That was just the problem. It was religion that made him so cruel—his concept of God.

Mark's father had noticed all the Old Testament texts admonishing the fear of the Lord. He figured that they meant that we ought to be frightened of the Almighty. So he determined through fear and intimidation to train his boys to be afraid of their Father in heaven. And the easiest way to enforce such a "fear of God" was to make them tremble before their father on earth.

Every morning he angrily stomped down the stairs as he woke up his boys. Mark can hardly think of a day when his father didn't flaunt his indignation. Not because anything had upset him, but because that was the way he pictured God, and so he communicated such wrath to his sons.

Unfortunately he succeeded all too well. Mark and his brother suffered deep damage emotionally and spiritually. Although fine students and hard workers, they lacked the confidence and social skills needed in order to thrive in life. Instead, they barely managed to survive.

Mark, someone I've come to know quite well, struggled with a fear of all authority figures, such as school principals and employers. Unable to relate well to his peers, he found his high school years cursed with loneliness. He compensated for his social isolation with scholastic brilliance, but that only alienated him further from fellow students.

Mark's mother was the finest of parents, tender and loving to her sons. Only her love preserved them from the follies of drugs and wild living. Yet her influence could only go so far.

Regrettably, Mark's pastors didn't provide much spiritual help. Not because they didn't care—they earnestly warned their congregations about denying the world's pleasures and striving to please God. Unfortunately, they portrayed God as a big general in the sky who expected absolute perfection of all saints, young and old. No excuses for weak human frailty.

Naturally Mark couldn't get any satisfaction from religion. By the time he graduated from high school he had given up on a relationship with God—it seemed to be an impossible burden piled on top of all of life's other duties. Yet he didn't want to divorce himself from God altogether, so he enrolled in a Christian college with the help of two scholarships he had earned.

Then, in his sophomore year, a friend introduced Mark to the little book *Steps to Christ*. This Christian classic explains in its first chapter how God is merciful and gracious, tenderhearted even to His enemies. It was quite a different picture of deity than Mark had grown up with.

Now he determined to get to the bottom of the truth about God. What does it really mean to "fear the Lord"? How can it harmonize with our love for the God who sacrificed Himself for our salvation?

Turning to the concordance in the back of his Bible, Mark looked up every text that mentioned the word *fear*. Several texts he ran across really surprised him, such as Proverbs 14:26: "In the fear of the Lord there is strong confidence, and His children will have a place of refuge."

How could that be—strong confidence in the fear of God? A place of refuge? Quite the opposite of what Mark had been trained to believe. He discovered that fearing God means respecting Him, putting our confidence in what He offers us instead of what the world promises.

Another text that helped to explain the fear of the Lord was Psalm 33:18: "Behold, the eye of the Lord is on those who fear Him, on those who hope in His mercy." Evidently fearing God means trusting in His mercy rather than in the counterfeit satisfaction of the world. So it is that "the fear of the Lord is to hate evil" (Proverbs 8:13).

All this was new indeed to Mark. In the New Testament he found more evidence that the fear of God does not mean being afraid of Him. Luke 1:74 says that God gave us Jesus so that we "might serve Him without fear."

Yes, it is true that God is a consuming fire to sin. But sinners who seek refuge in His gift of Jesus Christ find acceptance and adoption: "For you did not receive a spirit that makes you a slave again to fear, but you received the Spirit of sonship. And by Him [Jesus] we cry, 'Abba, Father'" (Romans 8:15, NIV).

The word *Abba* is an interesting one. Some would translate it "father," but Paul could have chosen a more formal word if that's what he wanted to say. Actually, "Abba" signifies an affectionate, familiar name for father —"Papa," "Daddy."

At first Mark shrank back from such familiarity with the omnipotent God. It seemed somehow irreverent. Then it dawned on him that the word *Abba* represented precisely the close paternal relationship he had been missing all his life. This was just what he desperately needed now to be healed from the scars of his youth.

The wonderful relationship we have with our "Abba" in heaven does more than merely meet our own needs—it's for God's sake too. He needs our love as well. In fact, He created us to satisfy an emotional hunger in His own heart. Up in heaven millions of angels, celestial beings, surrounded God, but He wanted to have some special children. That's why He made us, so we could bear His unique likeness: "So God created man in His own image, . . . male and female He created them" (Genesis 1:27).

Mark could hardly believe the glorious fact that we exist as human beings because of the longing God feels in His heart for us. He had always imagined that God could get along quite well alone. After all, you would think the Almighty could take care of Himself.

Really, though, this shouldn't be hard for us to understand. Husbands and wives enjoy each other and their many friends, yet still they feel loneliness for children. So they forfeit peace and prosperity for the privilege of hosting a screaming little red-faced dynamo—wet diapers and all! It's a human hunger to be parents, to have and to hold someone formed after our likeness. The craving to care for and laugh with one of our own.

Our children need the hugs and kisses we bestow upon them. But we crave their little hugs and kisses just as much. How would you feel if your little ones didn't hug you? We require our children just as much as they do us!

Now think about it—what does this tell us about God and His craving for our affection?

The reality of this marvelous truth didn't fully dawn on Mark until one morning in May of 1982. There, in the maternity room of the hospital, he held for the first time his own son, Jason. Words can't describe the feelings that thrilled his heart. He longed to lavish his love upon the little one and protect him from everything harmful and painful in the world.

Jason is growing up to be Daddy's boy. When he was 15 months old his mother went away to the hospital for three days for the birth of his sister. During that time Jason slept right on Mark's chest, heart to heart with his father.

When Mommy came home, eager to hold Jason again, nothing doing. He jumped off her lap and toddled over to Daddy. Needless to say, his father didn't mind it at all.

Mark's whole life is wrapped up in his son. They play ball together, walk to the store, go fishing. Everything possible they do together. He knows by experience what he means to God because of all that Jason is to him. The last remaining scars of Mark's sad childhood are being healed through his relationship with his son. God has used Jason to show Mark how a heavenly Father's heart yearns for each member of the human family.

One question, though, still troubled Mark about God's personal care for all of us—How could He possibly take individual notice of billions of human beings at the same time? And how could He hear the separate prayers of millions of Christians around the world, prayers that ascend to heaven all at once?

Then it dawned on him how such individual attention would be possible. At the office he has a favorite software package that enables his computer to run nine separate programs at the same time—with the same individual attention that any of those programs would receive from the computer even if it were the only one operating.

He realized that if a computer on earth can provide such individual attention to so many things at the same time, why couldn't the infinite God in heaven? Why couldn't His relationship with each Christian be as distinct and full as though there were not another on the face of the earth, not another one for whom He gave His beloved Son?

Yes, God is well able to hear the personal prayers of each of us at the same time. And did you ever stop to realize that He needs our fellowship in prayer just as we do? The main goal of prayer, even beyond asking for healing or food or whatever else, is to have a close and intimate relationship with our Father in heaven—for His sake as well as our own!

Think of Christ's parable of the prodigal son. While the young man lived it up in a far-off land, his father at home missed him. He waited there on the front porch, watching for his beloved boy to return home. One more proof here that God needs us just as we need Him, and that's why He made us.

How does that make you feel? Mark thought it was fantastic.

Our Creator spared nothing that could make His human children happy. Genesis 1 and 2 explains how He provided our world as a perfect paradise, beautiful beyond belief. Then He turned it over to Adam and Eve, giving them the ability to share their own love and populate the earth with happy children.

Imagine the idyllic paradise that Adam and Eve enjoyed together in their garden. Miles of green meadows carpeted with a rainbow array of flowers. Forests of fragrant trees with clear running streams. All kinds of animals, all friendly and tame.

Everything that could possibly delight our hearts, God gave us to enjoy with Him. Then every evening He came down to the garden to visit in an intimate way with Adam and Eve. As they talked and laughed together, they experienced a fulfilling relationship that was the highlight of life for them all.

The wonderful life Adam and Eve enjoyed with the Lord did have some risk, however. God created us with the freedom of personal choice, the power to love Him in return—or to withhold our love. The ability to obey—or to launch a rebellion.

Suppose God had created us without freedom of choice, like a locomotive rolling along the tracks, unable to choose its own path. No, He didn't want us riding the rails of His will without our consent. So He provided us the steering wheel of choice.

Naturally, any type of freedom can be abused, but God knew that personal choice is as essential as oxygen in providing an atmosphere where we can enjoy a loving relationship with Him. Then, to multiply our joy of living in His image, God took a further risk. He shared with us His powers of reproduction and responsibility, giving us dominion over His creation. This provided emotional fulfillment and accomplishment. But if the human race ever decided to abuse those twin privileges—the power of responsibility and freedom of choice—the whole world would plunge into perdition.

It would produce prisons and pollutants. Hospitals and arsenals. Missiles and caskets. Exactly what we see around us today. Sin has ruined everything.

You know how it happened. Adam and Eve chose to steer off God's highway of happiness, and they wrecked at a tree there in the Garden of Eden.

That tree provided the test of their love and loyalty. God asked them to stay away from it, assuring them that He had already lavished upon them everything that could make them happy. But if they ever wished to question His goodness and His plan for their happiness, they had opportunity to express that doubt and dissatisfaction at the tree.

The price of disobedience would be high, though. Death would result the very day they disobeyed (see Genesis 2:16, 17).

The punishment of death was not the reaction of an offended God retaliating against rebellious sinners. Rather, He is the source of life, and we must maintain our relationship with Him to sustain our lives. Separated from Him, we have no more hope for existence than a branch broken from the tree. That is why God would have to recognize rebellion by cutting off sinners from life.

At this point the plot thickens. God wasn't the only one eager to have the loyalty of Adam and Eve. The devil determined to rob the Creator of His human family by luring us away. He planned to tempt our first parents to doubt the Father's goodness, making them think He was withholding fulfillment from them.

This raises the question Where did the devil come from? The Bible says he began life as Lucifer, leader of heaven's angels. Angels too have the power of choice. Unfortunately, Lucifer exercised his free will by launching a rebellion. He actually attempted a takeover of God's throne. You can read the story of how Lucifer turned himself into the devil in Isaiah 14 and Ezekiel 28.

Jesus gave some interesting insight into the origin of evil. He called the devil the father of lies. Evidently Lucifer managed to plant seeds of doubt about God's goodness in the minds of the angels under his leadership (some of the same lies about God's love that Mark had grown up with). Through insinuations and subtle deceptions Lucifer managed to win over a third of the angels to his side. Then with his celestial army he attacked the throne of God.

Naturally, God could not permit such a tyrant to control the universe and bring about its ruin. He had to stop the rebellion, so He cast the rebels out of heaven.

Here we encounter another question. Why didn't God immediately destroy the devil and his angels? They would someday die anyway. Why not right away?

Let's consider this carefully. What would God's loyal angels have thought if they saw Him snuff out His enemies? They might have wondered whether some of Satan's charges had been right after all. Perhaps God simply overpowered His enemy to stop some ugly truth from coming out.

No wonder God didn't destroy the father of lies right away. Too many questions needed answers. Love for God survives only in minds convinced about His goodness, hearts touched by His kindness. Satan's troublesome questions interfered with the loyal angels' ability to trust God, to love Him. And remember, without such confidence in God's character, His government would cease to function. So for the good of the universe He allowed the devil opportunity to showcase his principles.

Satan claimed to have a better government, and now he had opportunity to prove it—right here on our planet before an onlooking universe.

Because God didn't want the enemy to harass the human race, however, He limited the devil's access to Adam and Eve to that single tree in the Garden of Eden. He warned them to stay away from it, lest they suffer the same fate as those fallen angels.

But one day something terrible happened. When God arrived for His daily special visit Adam and Eve were missing. Hiding. They had rebelled against their Creator and abandoned His plan for their happiness.

You probably know how it happened. Genesis 3 explains that Eve got curious and wandered over to the tree. Waiting for her was the serpent with his temptations. He managed to convince her that she could become a goddess if she disobeyed her Creator and followed him instead.

Eve believed the devil's lie. She took the fruit from the serpent's hands and ate. Adam, not wanting to be separated from his beautiful bride, joined her rebellion. And all the problems in our world today have resulted from that sad decision there in Eden, when our parents abandoned their heavenly Father and forfeited His plan for their lives.

Immediately they lost their innocence. Estranged from God, they ran away from Him. God arrived that evening to fellowship with them as usual, but they were hiding. Scared. Hadn't He warned that the same day they ate from that tree they would die? And here He came to kill them!

No, He had come to save them. A death did take place there at the gates of the Garden of Eden. God took an innocent animal and sacrificed it, with Adam and Eve watching. Then with the skin of that victim He clothed the guilty sinners.

What was happening? God was showing them that He meant what He said—sin brings death. But sinners don't have to die their own death. God would come down to earth and die for us on the cross. Here we see the good news of salvation communicated by God way back in Eden when He sacrificed that lamb.

So in a sense Adam and Eve did indeed die that day, through the death of that substitute lamb. Its blameless blood flowed on their behalf, pointing forward to Jesus, who would come here to lay down His life for us as God's sacrificial Lamb.

Yes, God had to be just. The execution of death must take place. But the Father wasn't willing to give up His beloved children. Instead, He would visit our sin-cursed planet and become our Saviour.

And so He did. Our Lord lived among us as a lonely man, poor and forsaken. His disciples imagined He would chase out the Roman occupation army and rule with a rod of iron. But Jesus seemed more interested in healing the sick, raising the dead, and preaching the gospel. They couldn't relate to Christ's humble style of ministry, and that left Him lonely.

The night before His death Jesus wanted to spend some quiet time alone with the disciples. Unfortunately, they were determined to pursue their frequent discussion about which of them was most important. Who would rule with greatest authority in the new kingdom? (See Luke 22:24.)

Later that evening, in the Garden of Gethsemane, Christ suffered a special kind of loneliness. Something He had never felt before—separation from His Father because of His identification with our sinfulness. Desperately needing the support of His closest disciples, He asked them to pray with Him. But they didn't seem too concerned, and soon fell asleep.

Three times Jesus came to them looking for some word of encouragement and support, but each time He found them sleeping. It was a great temptation to abort His rescue mission and go back to heaven.

After all, why not? His enemies were hurrying to arrest Him. His friends didn't care enough about themselves or about Him to stay awake and pray. How easy it would have been to slip away and leave us all to our doom. But He didn't.

Two gardens, Eden and Gethsemane. Adam and Eve decided in Eden to abandon God. Jesus decided in

Gethsemane not to abandon us, but to remain faithful unto death so we could have eternal life.

The next day, hanging on the cross, Christ suffered that terrible loneliness of separation from God. The psalmist echoed what must have been His feelings:

"Reproach has broken my heart, and I am so sick. And I looked for sympathy, but there was none, and for comforters, but I found none" (Psalm 69:20, NASB).

Have you ever looked for comfort but couldn't find anyone who cared? Then you can understand a little bit of how lonely Jesus felt. But nobody who ever lived experienced the depths of loneliness that He endured. It seemed He would forever be forsaken by the Father. None of us can fathom that ultimate abandonment that broke His heart when He cried, "My God, My God, why have You forsaken Me?" (Matthew 27:46).

Yes, God did have to abandon Jesus on the cross in order to accept us back into His family. On Calvary Jesus won back everything Adam and Eve had thrown away. Soon He will come again and restore Eden's paradise. If we entrust our lives to Him now, we'll live forever with Him then, never to be lonely again!

Good news indeed—God created us for fellowship with Him. More dearly than we yearn for human love, He craves our affection, our trust, our loyalty.

Have you been running away from your Father in heaven? Maybe you've been confused about how much God really cares about you, how deeply He loves you. Come home to His heart and you'll discover the most fulfilling relationship of your life.

If you are already a Christian, what kind of relationship do you have with God? Let Him be Abba, your Father, your Daddy!

If you want more:
> Psalm 27:10
> Psalm 103:13, 14
> Luke 15:11-32
> John 14:23
> 1 John 3:1-3

Chapter 7

Brian's Hope

The day began as just another February morning, cold and gray. Daddy kissed the family goodbye and drove off to work as the kids left for school. He would be home at 5:00 for supper. Afterward he had promised to take Brian to the basketball game. The sports-loving 12-year-old could hardly wait to spend the evening with his father.

But 5:00 came and went with no sign of Daddy. Supper began to get cold. Five-thirty. Brian started fretting—if Daddy didn't hurry home they would be late for the game.

When the 6:00 news began without her husband home yet, Brian's mother, Donna, became worried.

At 6:15 the phone rang. It was the hospital.

"Mrs. Taylor? Please come to the emergency room right away. Your husband has been in an accident."

Donna gasped. "Is he going to be all right?"

"He's in surgery right now. Come as soon as you can."

She left Brian and 10-year-old Laura with a neighbor and hurried the 15 miles to the hospital. On the dark highway up ahead she saw red flares and blinking orange lights. Could this be the place where it had happened?

It was! The tow truck was hoisting a blue Mazda— John's car. The vehicle was so smashed she could hardly recognize it.

Chills of horror raced up her spine as she sped on toward the hospital. After minutes that seemed like hours she finally arrived at the emergency room. Worried-looking nurses met her at the door.

The dreaded news tumbled out: head-on collision . . . drunken driver . . . less than a 50-50 chance.

Less than 50-50! Donna translated those cold odds into awful reality: The odds were that John would never take Brian to any more basketball games. It was less than likely that the kids would ever again bundle up with him for bedtime stories. She would probably sleep in an empty widow's bed the rest of her life.

"O God, where are You? Can You hear me up there?" her mind screamed.

With John hovering between life and death, she didn't dare leave the hospital. She felt guilty about not being with the kids when they needed her so much, even though she called them continually. The pastor's wife took them home from the neighbors' and spent the night with them.

Surgery lasted until nearly midnight. The weary doctor emerged from the operating room and told her, "We've done everything we can, but I can't promise you anything. Keep your fingers crossed."

I'll do better than that—I'll pray! Donna thought to herself. Throughout the endless night she maintained her lonely vigil in the waiting room. Morning dawned clear and bright, the darkest day of her life. Just about the time John would have normally left for work, he died.

That was it. Daddy was dead. Something inside Donna died too. She felt paralyzed, numb. Wherever God was, He could keep His distance now. No need to bother Him further.

Pastor Clark understood. He quietly helped her make the funeral arrangements without sermonizing to her about faith and bravery. Somehow the strength of his presence helped atone for God's apparent absence.

The terrible finality of John's death struck Donna while she was deciding which one of his suits he should wear in the casket. Right there in the bedroom closet she collapsed on her face and pounded her fists against the floor.

"You're cruel, God! Why didn't You take some drunkard out of the world instead of my John? Or maybe some tyrant. Why rob me of my husband, the father of my children?"

She screamed the same censures against God to the pastor next morning. Quietly he sat there listening. For 15 minutes Donna continued raging until she convulsed in tears. Finally she looked up and pleaded, "Pastor, I really need to know why this happened. Can you help me understand?"

"I don't have all the answers," he admitted. "But I can tell you this much. For thousands of years God has been suffering from this planet's rebellion, much more than you and I can begin to comprehend. He Himself lost a loved One at the cross. And it's because of Christ's death there that we have the assurance of life forever in a better land."

Donna nodded numbly.

"We both know John truly believed in Jesus," the minister continued. "He had his faults, as we all do. But he was a sincere Christian with his sins covered by the blood of Christ. When Jesus comes, He will raise John from death's sleep—and both of you will be together once more, never to part again."

Only weeks ago John and she had discussed the possibility of one of them dying. They promised each other that if it happened, the surviving spouse would remain faithful to God so that they could be united again in eternity.

Donna apologized to the pastor for her thunderstorm of rage and grief. "I—I shouldn't be bitter with God. He's not the one who got the other driver drunk. Besides, I can't stay mad at the Lord—I need Him now more than ever."

"Don't be too hard on yourself, Donna," Pastor Clark said. "You are going through a grief process that psychologists say every sorrowing person suffers. Let me describe these stages of grief:

"First come shock and disbelief, denial of what happened. But sooner or later, loved ones must come to terms with their loss. That sparks an outburst of emotional release—like your experience in the bedroom closet and your talk with me today. Now you can expect various physical distresses, such as a lack of appetite, along with all kinds of emotional turmoil. And in the days and weeks ahead you will suffer lots of loneliness, interrupted by attacks of sheer panic."

It was her turn to listen silently now.

"Grieving widows often blame themselves for not having been perfect wives. They suffer resentment toward God, they feel angry toward other women who still have their husbands—they even may resent their own husbands for abandoning them."

"Why, that's terrible!" she objected. "I would never feel that way toward John—it wasn't his fault that he died."

"I'm not saying you will have that particular experience, Donna, but many widows do."

That puzzled her. "Christians shouldn't have all those bad feelings, should they?"

"Being a Christian doesn't mean we don't have human feelings," the pastor explained. "Especially during a crisis such as you are going through. When death comes unexpectedly and the loved one was especially close, as you and John were, the grieving process is all the more painful.

"No less a spiritual giant than C. S. Lewis suffered greatly in his time of personal grief. I brought along his book for you, *A Grief Observed*. Listen how he describes his experience:

"Tonight all the hells of young grief have opened again; the mad words, the bitter resentment, the fluttering in the stomach, the nightmare unreality, the wallowed-in tears."*

Donna sighed. "Well, if even C. S. Lewis went through all that, I guess I'm in good company."

"How true! Thousands, probably millions, of Christians all over the world are grieving just as you are right now. And God is close to every one of them. He understands how you hurt. He's been with you all through this heart-wrenching experience, and He won't forsake you now.

"You can't escape the suffering of grief. But you can get help from God whenever you feel like you're falling apart. Listen to this promise from His Word: 'Do not fear, for I am with you; do not be dismayed, for I am your God. I will strengthen you and help you; I will uphold you with my righteous right hand. . . . For I am the Lord, your God, who takes hold of your right hand and says to you, Do not fear; I will help you' [Isaiah 41:10-13, NIV]."

"Just what I needed to hear today," she said slowly. "Let me mark that text in my Bible."

Pastor Clark waited while she located the passage and highlighted it.

"One more thing, Donna. Don't expect yourself to understand everything about John's death—just trust those hands that were nailed to the cross for you. God will somehow work out everything for good. Then someday in heaven you will understand it all. Meanwhile, keep pouring out your heart to Jesus—He's got big shoulders to cry on, you know."

"Thank you, Pastor," she replied, managing a smile through her tears. After they prayed together, she felt better. Now she could face the funeral and think about helping the kids cope.

The next day, Friday morning, Donna sat between Brian and Laura in the funeral home waiting for John's service to begin. As the organ played softly, her mind filled with pictures, memories. Their wedding. Moving across the country to California. Brian and Laura being born. John and she getting baptized together.

They had so many memories, so many plans for the future. But now those plans themselves were memories. A fresh wave of grief overwhelmed her.

Just then the service started, opening with a beautiful song about heaven. Pastor Clark stepped up to the pulpit. Wiping a tear, he opened his Bible and read from the words of Jesus in John 14. Donna leaned forward—it had been one of her husband's favorite chapters:

"'Let not your heart be troubled; you believe in God, believe also in Me. In My Father's house are many mansions:

. . . I go to prepare a place for you. And if I go and prepare a place for you, I will come again and receive you to Myself; that where I am, there you may be also' [John 14:1-3]."

Then the minister laid down his Bible and began to speak, straight from his heart:

"God had a wonderful purpose in creating the human family in His image. But Adam and Eve abandoned heaven's plan for their happiness, thus polluting paradise with pain and death. Then God in His love took action to save our doomed planet in rebellion. Jesus came down here 'so that by his death he might destroy him who holds the power of death—that is, the devil—and free those who all their lives were held in slavery by their fear of death' [Hebrews 2:14, 15, NIV].

"When Christ rose from the tomb, He conquered the power of death. 'Where, O death, is your victory? Where, O death, is your sting?' [1 Corinthians 15:55, NIV]. Soon He will come again, and He will bring with Him the keys of death to set free every one of His children held in death's dark prison. Nothing on earth matters more than this blessed hope."

The pastor paused, then continued:

"I got to know John pretty well these past several years, and I can testify that nothing was more important to him than meeting Jesus with his family. Why, just last week, Tuesday night, John and I conducted a Bible study in a new believer's home. He shared the apostle Paul's description of what will happen when Jesus comes for His people."

Donna listened intently as Pastor Clark read the description of Christ's return in 1 Thessalonians 4:16-18, hearing the words with new meaning: "'For the Lord himself will come down from heaven, with a loud command, with the voice of the archangel and with the trumpet call of God, and the dead in Christ will rise first. After that, we who are still alive and are left will be caught up with them in the clouds to meet the Lord in the air. And so we will be with the Lord forever. Therefore encourage each other with these words' [NIV]."

The pastor looked directly at her and Brian and Laura as he concluded, "And so the Word of God offers us bright hope on this dark day of grief. The Lord Jesus Christ will pierce the heavens with a mighty shout that resounds around the world. The graves will surrender their captives. John will come forth to be together with his precious family, never to be separated again. What comfort for our hearts today!"

Donna needed some comforting as they lowered John's casket into the cold earth. She nearly fainted with grief. But many loving arms and the precious promises of Scripture sustained her.

John's parents, present at the funeral, were not believers. They cried empty, hacking sobs of hopelessness. It was a startling contrast with the warm and tearful hugs of hope Donna got from her Christian brothers and sisters. The assurance of Jesus' return made all the difference.

That night Donna and the kids cuddled together on the big bed, just as they always had done when Daddy read them stories. They cried a bit, hugged a lot, and talked until 11:00.

Then Brian came up with an idea. "Mom, let's imagine what it will be like to go to heaven with Daddy."

She hugged her son tightly. Of all the family, Brian probably needed John the most. Just about to enter his teenage years, he had had a close and affectionate relationship with his father. The boy craved the assurance that he and his daddy would be together again some day.

Donna reached for the family Bible and read Revelation 1:7. "Every eye will see Jesus coming, son," she added. "Then Daddy's grave will burst open, and before we know it, he'll be right there with us! Suddenly we'll find ourselves floating upward, away from the smog and the smoke choking this old earth. Together we're going to sail through the stars up to heaven."

Now Laura perked up. "That's going to be some space trip! What will happen when we get to heaven, Mommy?"

"There will be quite a welcome waiting—God the Father will greet us. Angels will crowd around us. We'll enjoy a homecoming banquet better than any Thanksgiving dinner we've had on earth. And our mansion will be more magnificent than we can even begin to imagine."

"Mom!" Her son's eyes brightened for the first time since the tragedy. "Daddy won't have to go off to work anymore—we can be together all the time. Think of the fun we can have up there with him. A canoe trip down the river of life. We'll float 200 miles and camp out every evening for a week."

Laura squealed with delight. "Daddy and Jesus will build me a water slide behind our mansion. A great big slide one mile long. And I'm going to have all my friends over to play on it."

Now Donna caught their eager spirit. "You know how Daddy loved frozen yogurt. Jesus will give us our own frozen yogurt machine with six different flavors. And we'll enjoy as much as we want to eat without getting fat. It won't even cost anything!"

Then she found Revelation 21 in the Bible and read the first several verses to the children. "You see, after we have been in heaven for a while, Jesus will re-create this earth— make it all new again for us. The prophet Isaiah says that in this new earth we'll have a home in the country."

"Plus our mansion in the holy city!" Brian interjected.

"That's right, son. Our city mansion will be built for us by Jesus—it's probably ready for us now. The country home we ourselves will build with Daddy. There will be acres of beautiful flowers with all the colors of the rainbow. Maybe a forest of fragrant redwoods with clear running streams."

Brian's eyes got even bigger. "Let's plan what we want in our new earth home. How about an indoor waterfall! And a golf course with the greenest grass you ever saw—you know how Daddy loved to play golf. He promised to teach me how—and he will, after Jesus resurrects him."

Laura piped up, "I want a stable of Arabian horses. And my own zoo—without bars, since the animals will be tame. How loud do you think my lions will purr?"

Hugging her, Donna continued, "Even learning will be fun in the future, believe it or not. The angels will explain fascinating secrets of science. And you can travel with your favorite friends on field trips around the universe. You'll have your old friends from earth, and make new friends with kids you've never met before—even ones from Bible times."

"My best friend will be Queen Esther," Laura predicted.

"And mine will be David," Brian declared. "I want him to teach me how to use a slingshot!"

Donna laughed, then became serious. "Kids, do you remember that talk Daddy had with us last summer when we visited Grandma's grave? He asked us to promise him that we will always be faithful to God. That way we will all be ready when Jesus comes."

"I'm going to be faithful, just as Daddy was," Brian resolved.

"Me too," Laura added solemnly.

Their mother held them close, and they prayed together. Then they turned out the light.

Soon Donna heard the rhythmic breathing of the children, peacefully sleeping. Her mind raced on as she tried to picture what heaven might offer for adults. No more bills. No more rat race. No more disappointments and little disagreements.

John and she would again have a wonderful relationship in heaven. They could have a little hideaway cabin in the forest just for the two of them. Soon she found herself actually smiling there in that darkened bedroom. For the first time since John's death she knew that the family would manage to make it without him. Life would be tough—there would always be an emptiness—but the three of them would survive, thanks to God's help.

Then something Brian had said that evening came back to her. With wisdom beyond his years he had exclaimed, "How exciting for us to be alive now on earth—it's like a ball game in the bottom of the ninth inning! We'll be right here when God wins the game."

It was quite a challenge and opportunity. And yes, what a hope—Brian's hope.

Donna drifted off to sleep with the children. One morning they would all awaken to a new day with Jesus—and Daddy. Lonely no longer!

If you want more:
>   Isaiah 35:10
>   Matthew 24
>   Titus 2:11-14
>   1 Peter 1:3-9
>   Revelation 22

---

* C. S. Lewis, *A Grief Observed* (New York: Bantam Books, 1961), pp. 66, 67.

Chapter 8

Alice
the Abandoned

Remember Alice? We met her in our introduction to this book. Let's get better acquainted with her.

She's a widow, you recall. Early one morning several years ago her husband, Karl, went out to milk the cows. He never came back in for breakfast. There in the barn he suffered a massive heart seizure and died instantly.

Just that suddenly, after nearly 50 years of togetherness, Alice found herself alone. Karl had planned to sell their farm and take her on a well-earned vacation, a golden anniversary tour of Europe. Now she had to dispose of the farm by herself and find an apartment.

She moved to the city where two of her children lived with their families, hoping they would keep her company a bit. But no, it turned out they had no time for her. When she calls to see how they are doing, she always seems to be interrupting some favorite TV program. While she understands that they are busy, just once in a while, wouldn't they enjoy a home-cooked meal with Mother? Alice gazes fondly at their pictures night after night. She never imagined that she would become a bother to her own family.

It wasn't fair. She had been a faithful Christian mother, training up her children in the right way. Now they don't even attend church regularly. Her friends have told her that she should quit being so burdened about them, but that's not the way the Lord made mothers. How can a mother not care?

Self-pity tempts her at times, but she refuses to succumb. Instead, she has immersed herself in community service projects and activities for senior citizens.

Every Friday her best friend, Mabel, used to pick her up for lunch at the Windmill Restaurant. Alice never realized how much Mabel meant to her until suddenly her friend had a stroke. Within a week she died.

Death is the harshest fact of life. Just in the past three years, five of Alice's good friends have died, besides her husband. She feels like the sole survivor of a catastrophe. But she hasn't become bitter. God has been good to her. Her time of loneliness, being such a new experience, in itself reminds Alice of how full her life had been through the years.

God has lots of comfort for lonely people in His Word. Through her well-worn Bible, Alice has come closer than ever to His heart of love. Her eyes are clouding up and she can't read as much as she used to, but she still studies and prays every day.

One morning last spring she fell and broke her ankle. That meant she couldn't make it to her church for Easter Sunday services. "Oh, well," she told herself, "I'll just stay home and watch some good sermons on the Resurrection."

One of those Easter sermons offered her more than she expected. The preacher read from 1 Corinthians 15: "'For as in Adam all die, so also in Christ all shall be made alive. But each in his own order: Christ the first fruits, after that those who are Christ's at His coming' [verses 22, 23]." [1]

Alice had memorized the passage many years ago in Sunday school. But now something she never noticed before dawned on her. Something downright startling. The Bible says that those who belong to Jesus will be made alive at His coming! Not when they die, but at His return.

That was news indeed to her. She had always believed that the dead are not really dead, but continue to exist outside their bodies either in heaven or in hell. Now this text challenged that assumption. Could it really be that when people die they simply wait in their graves until Jesus comes?

Her mind groped for understanding as the preacher continued in 1 Corinthians 15: " 'Behold, I tell you a mystery; we shall not all sleep, but we shall all be changed, in a moment, in the twinkling of an eye, at the last trumpet; for the trumpet will sound, and the dead will be raised imperishable, and we shall be changed. For this perishable must put on imperishable, and this mortal must put on immortality' [verses 51-53]."

Evidently death was a sleep that lasts till the resurrection. When the trumpet sounds at Christ's coming, millions of tombs will burst open. Then the saints who are watching the dead come to life will find their own bodies instantly transformed into perfection and immortality.

Alice had heard dozens of sermons proclaiming a secret rapture to take place in the twinkling of an eye. Now she learned that it's the re-creation of our bodies—not a secret rapture—that happens in the twinkling of an eye.

"This is marvelous!" she mused to herself. "One moment I'll be standing there with my gray hair and arthritis, and the next moment I'll be bouncing around in eternal health and youth!"

That Easter morning Alice had only intended to enjoy an inspiring sermon, but she also discovered the truth about the resurrection. It seemed so strange, though, so different from what she had always believed. New questions flooded her mind. Part of her wanted to brush them aside and hold on to what she had always been taught. She was too old to change her beliefs, wasn't she?

But down deep Alice knew better—the patriarch Abraham was even older than she when God called him to forsake his homeland and move away. He obeyed by faith, and Alice knew she must do the same. Friends might think she was going senile with her new convictions, but God's Word mattered more than people's opinions.

Alice resolved to study the subject through. Hobbling over to her bookshelf, she pulled out her big blue concor-

dance, which arranged every word of the Bible in alphabet-
ical order. With her magnifying glass she went down the list
of texts under "death" and "dead" and "die." Here's two
examples of what she came up with:

"For the living know they will die; but the dead do not
know anything" (Ecclesiastes 9:5).

"The dead do not praise the Lord, nor do any who go
down into silence" (Psalm 115:17).

It amazed her to discover that the dead are not in
heaven praising the Lord. Instead, she realized, they are
sleeping in silence until they awake at the resurrection: "So
man lies down and does not rise. Until the heavens be no
more, he will not awake nor be aroused out of his sleep"
(Job 14:12).

But what about all those sermons she had heard
insisting that the soul travels to heaven at death? Alice
searched and searched, but nothing in the Bible said
anything like that. What she learned about the soul was
quite different: "Then the Lord God formed man of dust
from the ground, and breathed into his nostrils the breath
of life; and man became a living soul" (Genesis 2:7). [2]

Evidently we human beings do not *have* souls—instead,
we *are* souls. In the beginning God breathed life into man's
body and he became a living soul. At death, the opposite of
creation happens. "His spirit [breath] departs, he returns to
the earth; in that very day his thoughts perish" (Psalm
146:4).

"Well," she concluded, "the Old Testament seems clear
enough that the dead are asleep in their graves. But what
about the New Testament?" She recalled the words of Jesus,
"I go to prepare a place for you. And if I go and prepare a
place for you, I will come again, and receive you to Myself;
that where I am, there you may be also" (John 14:2, 3).

So Jesus promised to prepare a place in heaven, then He
would return to earth in order that His disciples could be
with Him. How could that be if they had already gone to
heaven at death?

The popular teaching about death now made no sense,
Alice realized. It would be as if she traveled to New York to

visit her niece and be welcomed with the words "Auntie, make yourself at home. Now excuse me for a few days while I go back to Ohio so I can pick you up to be here in New York with me."

Ridiculous, wouldn't you say? Alice thought so. Only if the saints were sleeping in their graves would Jesus need to return to earth to get them. She remembered that Christ referred to death as a sleep in John 11. So the dead were really dead after all, unconscious and at rest until the resurrection.

After she had thought about it awhile, Alice decided that it really was better that way. How would a mother enjoy looking down from heaven at her funeral service, seeing her children crying for her? Then watching them trying to cook and clean without even being able to help them?

No! Heaven wouldn't be fun at all under such circumstances. It was much better for all to go up together when Jesus came.

The more she pondered the Bible teaching about death, the more she felt relieved, especially when she considered hellfire. Her husband, good and honest though he was, never took an interest in the Bible. As far as Alice knew, Karl had died as a lost man outside of Christ. Consequently she had often thought of him as being in hell, writhing about in torment. Now she knew he was asleep in his grave awaiting the great judgment of the last day. What the Bible described seemed a lot more fair than what she had been taught.

Suppose Hitler had gone to hell in 1945 after murdering millions, and met Cain, who killed only his brother, Abel, yet had already been tormented in the flames for thousands of years. Should Cain go to hell thousands of years before Hitler just because he happened to live at an earlier time in earth's history?

That wouldn't seem right! And here's something else: We get upset at the thought of someone being sentenced without a trial. Would God send lost people to hell before their day in court? Or would He punish sinners for centuries only to call them up on judgment day to see whether they were really guilty?

What kind of God do we have? Something's wrong there, wouldn't you say? Alice thought so. She determined to get to the bottom of this matter of death, hell, and the resurrection.

One afternoon an invitation arrived in the mail for something called a Revelation Seminar. She had always avoided the book of Revelation with its strange imagery and fearsome beasts, but now as she read the brochure she sensed that here might be the answer to her questions.

When Alice phoned for information about registering, she spoke with Pastor Smith, the seminar leader, a bright and friendly young man fresh out of college. He explained that the book of Revelation was nothing to be scared of—it was actually the "Revelation of Jesus Christ." Then he offered to arrange a ride for her every Tuesday and Thursday evening. She gladly accepted.

Alice felt right at home at the seminar, never missing a night. Her heart thrilled with all kinds of new discoveries in God's Word. Especially fascinating to her were the events immediately following the resurrection foretold in Revelation 20. Pastor Smith had the class read verse 6: "Blessed and holy is the one who has a part in the first resurrection; over these the second death has no power, but they will be priests of God and of Christ and will reign with Him for a thousand years."

"This 1,000-year time span is also known as the millennium," he pointed out. "The first resurrection, the raising of believers when Jesus returns, marks the beginning of the millennium. Then after those 1,000 years the resurrection of those who rejected Jesus takes place.

"Notice verse 5: 'The rest of the dead did not come to life until the thousand years were completed.' The unsaved are resurrected to face judgment and the second and final death."

Alice raised her hand. "Why would God wait 1,000 years?"

Pastor Smith had a reasonable answer waiting, as usual. "God won't punish the wicked until all the universe fully understands why—until you and I understand. So the apostle Paul speaks of a time when 'the saints will judge the world' [1 Corinthians 6:2]. This happens during our 1,000 years in heaven, according to verse 4 here in Revelation 20.

"You see, Alice, God will open the books of record to us, and we'll have plenty of time for asking any question on our minds. Down here, life often appears to make no sense at all—when all the while God is working all things for our good. He will make everything plain to us in heaven. Then we will finally comprehend what we must now accept by faith."

It all made sense to Alice. She already had drawn up a mental list of things she wanted to ask the Lord up there.

Pastor Smith continued: "Jesus said everything hidden on earth now will be revealed in the future [see Luke 12:2]. Our important questions will be answered, and our curious questions, too. Think how fascinating it will be to learn the secrets of history. Secrets of the White House, the Kremlin, and the Mafia. Secrets of the pharaohs, the caesars, and the popes.

"When we get to heaven and look around, new questions will occur to us. Like, Where's my Bible class teacher? I thought he was such a sincere man—why didn't he make it?"

A man in the class remarked, "Some we thought were saved will be missing up there, and others we judged as lost will be saved."

"That's right," the pastor agreed. "Didn't Jesus say many of the first will be last and the last first? God will take the time to open it all to our understanding. We will see how He has indeed done everything possible to save each soul throughout human history. When all our questions have received their answers in heaven, we will be prepared to witness the sad day at the end of the 1,000 years when the unsaved will be punished."

Someone else in class asked, "During this millennium, what will be happening down here on earth?"

Pastor Smith explained that our planet will be empty. He read the words of the prophet Jeremiah: " 'I looked on the earth, and behold, it was formless and void; and to the heavens, and they had no light. . . . I looked, and behold, there was no man, and all the birds of the heavens had fled. I looked, and behold, the fruitful land was a wilderness, and all its cities were pulled down before the Lord, before His fierce anger. For thus says the Lord, "The whole land shall be a desolation, yet I will not execute a complete destruction" ' [Jeremiah 4:23-27].

"Evidently no human life remains after Jesus comes," he observed. "Only Satan and his angels are down here, roaming the ruins they brought upon the universe by their rebellion. Quite a gloomy scene, but did you notice the ray of hope? God promises that He would not make a final end to life on earth. Apparently He still has plans for our planet. Notice verses 7 and 8 in Revelation 20:

" 'And when the thousand years are completed, Satan will be released from his prison, and will come out to deceive the nations which are in the four corners of the earth, Gog and Magog, to gather them together for the war; the number of them is like the sand of the seashore.'

"So Satan will have his wicked followers back on this earth after the millennium."

"What happens next?" Nancy, one of Alice's new friends in the class, wanted to know.

"After the resurrection of the lost, things take place quite quickly. The devil assumes charge of his new army of rebels. Verse 9 unfolds the drama: 'And they came up on the broad plain of the earth and surrounded the camp of the saints and the beloved city, and fire came down from heaven and devoured them.' "

Now Alice raised her hand. "But how did the Holy City get down here? Weren't we up in heaven with Jesus?"

The pastor paused a moment. "Alice, the answer is so incredible, you wouldn't believe it if you didn't see it in God's Word. Look at Revelation 21:1-3: 'And I saw a new heaven and a new earth; for the first heaven and the first earth had passed away, and there is no longer any sea. And

I saw the holy city, new Jerusalem, coming down out of heaven from God, made ready as a bride adorned for her husband. And I heard a loud voice from the throne, saying, "Behold, the tabernacle of God is among men, and He shall dwell among them, and they shall be His people, and God Himself shall be among them." '

"Can you imagine what it will be like to travel from heaven back to earth and watch as the Holy City comes down? According to the Old Testament prophet Zechariah, Christ will stand that day upon the Mount of Olives just outside the ruins of present Jerusalem. His feet will divide the mountain into a great plain on which the New Jerusalem will rest [See Zechariah 14:3, 4]."

Now Alice understood what Jesus meant in the Beatitudes: "Blessed are the gentle, for they shall inherit the earth." Not this present polluted old planet. We will inherit a new earth, pure and unpolluted, following our 1,000 years in heaven.

"After the Holy City has settled on this earth," Pastor Smith continued, "everyone who has ever lived will be alive at the same time—inside or outside the New Jerusalem."

Alice tried to imagine the sight as Satan compared his vast army with the much smaller group within the city. He would have military leaders from all history behind him. There would probably be Hitler, along with famous generals who had never lost a battle. Satan would rally his forces for a final furious attack on God's throne in the Holy City. The huge army of rebels would move forward.

Then what would happen? Hellfire. Fire would pour down from heaven and devour the wicked. The earth would become a boiling lake of flame.

Pastor Smith pointed to an interesting parallel between the Flood destroying the world in Noah's day and the fire bringing on our planet's final destruction.

"Just as Noah's ark rode upon the waters of the Flood," he explained, "the Holy City with the saints inside will withstand the lake of fire. Hellfire will be hot—so hot that sin and sinners will not survive. But after those flames have done their cleansing work, they will go out. Remember how the water receded in Noah's day and the ark settled back down on the earth? Well, the lake of fire will subside like that, and the Holy City will rest upon a purified planet.

"Keep in mind that back in Noah's day when the people drowned, they were gone. God didn't keep them endlessly thrashing about in the water. And the citizens of ancient Sodom and Gomorrah aren't still burning, over there beneath the Dead Sea."

Someone interrupted, "But Pastor, doesn't the Bible say Sodom and Gomorrah were destroyed by 'eternal fire'? Right there in Jude 1:7 we find that those cities were 'exhibited as an example, in undergoing the punishment of eternal fire.' "

"Eternal fire in its effect," Smith explained. "You see, the punishment is everlasting—but not the punishing. Remember, the wages of sin is death, not eternal life in hell. Death means the absence of life, the absence of existence. So the doctrine of eternal hell isn't based upon Scripture. It's tradition. A holdover from ancient pagan beliefs."

Alice couldn't resist voicing her new convictions on the subject. "If God would punish my Karl in the flames for as long as He'd punish Hitler, He wouldn't be a God of justice! Suppose our court system sentenced every offender with the same jail term, shoplifters and murderers alike. None of us would like that—but that is exactly what I hear all the time about hell. Some people say all sinners will burn in the flames together as long as time shall last, even though some are more guilty than others. That just wouldn't be fair, and God won't do it!"

Pastor Smith couldn't resist a smile. "That's quite a convincing sermon out of you, Alice. And you're right— eternal torment doesn't make sense, in addition to being unbiblical.

"Here's another point to consider," he added. "On the cross Jesus paid the wages of the whole world's sin by His death. Did He suffer eternal torment? Of course not. Then to say that sinners must be eternally punished suggests that Jesus failed to pay the full price of their sin. And we know that's not true!

"So those who reject their Saviour's death must finally themselves perish. For the good of the universe, for the good of everyone concerned, every trace of sin will be erased. God's eternal kingdom of peace will reign at last."

At this point a young woman in the class raised her hand. "But what does the Bible mean about the smoke of their torment ascending up forever?"

"That's an important question," the pastor affirmed. "We must let the Bible interpret its own terms. Did you know the Scriptures use the word 'forever' more than 50 times for things already ended? For instance, in 1 Samuel 1:22 we read that the prophet Samuel's mother promised him as a gift to the Lord 'forever.' Yet verse 28 explains, 'As long as he lives he is dedicated to the Lord.'

"So there we have it. As long as the wicked live, as long as consciousness lasts, they will burn. For some it may be just a few moments. Others may suffer longer. Yet even Satan himself will be finished off at last. [3]

"Then God brings beauty out of ashes, re-creating the breathtaking beauty of long-lost Eden. Finally the rebellion will be over, never to trouble a peaceful universe again. Sin will be gone, and with it death and disappointment and pain. God will give this born-again planet to His people as our eternal paradise home."

Someone raised the question "Why would God move the capital city of the universe from heaven down to our little planet?"

"Because we are His precious people," the pastor responded. "You know the text 'God so loved the world, that He gave His only begotten Son' to us. Jesus was not a loan to the human race. He was a gift, and He still belongs to us today. For all eternity our Saviour will be one of the human family, our Brother as well as our Lord!

"And the earth, where Jesus suffered and died for our salvation, will be the place of God's eternal throne. Throughout endless ages the citizens of the universe will worship there with us on our world made new."

By now it was 8:30, time for the seminar to dismiss. On the way home Alice remarked, "All this is wonderful—too good not to be true, I'd say. Back when I broke my ankle and couldn't go to church for Easter, little did I dream that the Lord was opening the door to a whole new world of truth!"

She can hardly wait for the beginning of God's great eternity. How about you?

If you want more:

    Psalm 115:17

    Ezekiel 18:20

    Luke 14:14

    John 11:11-14

    2 Timothy 4:6-8

---

[1] All texts in this chapter come from the *New American Standard Bible*.

[2] Margin reading.

[3] You might have all kinds of questions about heaven and hell. Why not discuss them with the person who gave you this book? Or take a moment and write to me. I'll be happy to try answering your questions, and I'll send along a gift book you might enjoy.

Give me several weeks to get back to you, since I travel a lot, especially during the summer. I'd really enjoy hearing from you. Here's my address:

Martin Weber

C/o *It Is Written* telecast

Box O

Thousand Oaks, California 91320

Chapter 9

Noble's Dungeon Palace

W**ould you mind coming with us to headquarters?"** the policemen politely asked the young Christian. "We'll only keep you five minutes."

Those five minutes turned out to be 22 years—more than two decades of imprisonment and torture under conditions that cannot be described in this book. The crime? Faith in the Lord Jesus Christ.

If Noble Alexander had just kept quiet about Jesus and lived his faith silently, his government would have left him alone. But no, the 28-year-old lay preacher insisted on traveling around the country leading others to Jesus.

He had already received warnings, so it came as no surprise when the secret police arrested him. They accused him of subversive activities, labeling him a *plantado*— rebel against the government.

Noble remained confined in a loathsome prison until 1984, when presidential candidate Jesse Jackson negotiated his release and deportation to America. Newspapers here reported that Noble had been a spiritual leader among his fellow prisoners, organizing them into an underground prayer group.

Every day at noon Noble and his friends skipped lunch for the sake of spiritual food. It was quite a mixed group worshiping together: Catholics, Baptists, Pentecostals, and Seventh-day Adventists.

A Seventh-day Adventist, Noble led the Protestant services. The next day a Catholic prisoner would conduct worship in his tradition. Always they had a lookout to protect their privacy.

Noble managed to smuggle a Bible into the prison. The inmates shared it by tying it to a string and pulling it through cracks in the cell walls. Several well-chosen hiding places concealed the precious Book from the guards. Then one day prison authorities got word about Noble's Bible and tried to confiscate it. The inmates quickly hid it in one of their special places. The guards beat and tortured Noble, but all he would tell them was "It's my Bible, and I'm never going to give it up!"

Naturally the guards didn't appreciate such stubborn commitment to Christ. They put him in their dungeon, a totally dark cell so narrow he had room only to lie down. A small slit in the door allowed "food" to be pushed inside.

Noble spent two years in that dark hole, his only companions vermin. The loneliness was terrible, but he had Jesus with him, and that was good enough to carry him through.

Recently I had the privilege of meeting Noble Alexander. I wondered what he would be like. After all he had suffered, I expected him to wear a halo of somberness. Was I ever surprised! That man is one of the most cheerful, delightful people I've ever met. He laughed and laughed about how the prisoners hid the Bible from the guards, and about how wonderful it felt while in the dungeon to know his Bible had escaped confiscation.

I could tell you more about Noble's ordeal for Christ, but much of what he suffered is not fit for print. Suffice it to say that he finds living conditions in America more pleasant and healthy than those of the dungeon.

Noble lives in Massachusetts now, working for the Adventist Church. His thrilling testimony draws thousands into a deeper commitment to Christ. He is especially thankful for our land of freedom, where he can share his love for Jesus without fear or threat from government.

All of us can thank God for a legal system that requires our judges to be fair. If they harbor a bias against the accused, our constitution demands they be disqualified. Yet believe it or not, the ancient Hebrew legal code went even further to protect the rights of the defendant.

During Old Testament times the defense of the accused was a duty so sacred that the judge refused to delegate that job to an attorney. He himself served as the protector of the accused. *The Jewish Encyclopedia* explains that "attorneys at law are unknown in Jewish law." [1]

Their legal understanding required judges to "lean always to the side of the defendant" and to give him "the advantage of every possible doubt." [2]

Witnesses of the crime pressed charges, while the judge promoted the case of the defendant, biased in favor of acquittal. [3]

Only when overwhelmed by the evidence would the judge abandon his defense of the accused and reluctantly pronounce condemnation.

Lessons from the Hebrew law court abound for us today. A lot of Christians are frightened about facing God as their judge. If they only understood the biblical meaning of judgment, they would then realize that He is on our side! He personally takes upon Himself the job of our defense!

But if God is defending us in the heavenly judgment, who is accusing us? You guessed it—the devil. The Bible calls him the "accuser of the brethren" who "accuses them before God day and night" (Revelation 12:10, NASB). Apparently Satan is jealous about our going to heaven, where he used to live when he was Lucifer, prince of the angels. And so he charges God's children with being unfit to pass through the pearly gates.

But we are unworthy, aren't we? How do we counter his accusations?

Notice verse 11 in Revelation 12: "And they overcame him because of the blood of the Lamb" (NASB).

It's through the blood of Jesus that you and I overcome the devil's accusations. God can't deny Satan's contention that we are sinful. But in the blood shed on Calvary's cross

He finds the evidence He needs to pronounce us innocent. So He dismisses Satan's charges, endorsing the security in Christ we have enjoyed since we accepted Him.

In certain situations the Hebrew judge appointed an advocate to assist him in defending the accused. *The Jewish Encyclopedia* states that the husband could represent his wife and help the judge defend her if the verdict involved his personal rights. [4]

Here we have a glorious parallel with the heavenly judgment. Christ, Bridegroom of the church, purchased us with His precious blood. Now He serves as our court-appointed advocate to help the Father defend us from Satan—and to uphold His own right to take us to heaven and share His home with us forever.

God in the judgment takes our side against Satan. Jesus our advocate assists Him by interceding for us. The Father finds in the sacrifice of His Son the legal basis to accept repenting sinners and count us perfect.

I like that, don't you? It makes me feel confident in Christ about my salvation!

Let me share a simple experience from my days as a pastor to illustrate how Christ's sacrifice on Calvary enables us to pass heaven's judgment.

One summer day our pastoral staff went out of the office for a special planning session. We boarded the Amtrak train in Santa Ana bound for San Diego, had lunch down there, then came back. Believe it or not, we actually accomplished some work as the train skimmed the beautiful Pacific coastline.

Along the way, the conductor came around to see who was worthy to ride his train. While his investigative judgment went on, we felt no threat to secure passage—all of us had tickets. We knew the conductor wouldn't disqualify us because of our failures in life, or accept us because of our successes. His only question was "May I see your ticket?"

Likewise in God's judgment. What matters is whether or not we have Jesus. When we repent of our sins and accept Him as our Saviour, He is our ticket to heaven: "He who believes in Him is not judged; he who does not believe has been judged already, because he has not believed in the name of the only begotten Son of God" (John 3:18, NASB).

Our personal worthiness doesn't even deserve consideration in heaven's judgment—all hope of human merit collapsed during the judgment of our world at the cross (see John 12:31, 32). Calvary established a new standard of righteousness—salvation in Jesus. Today, when we forsake our sins in order to accept His gift, God accepts us in Christ. We can rejoice because our names are recorded in heaven's book of life.

However, this is not what people refer to "as once saved, always saved." Amtrak passengers must not throw away their tickets, or they disqualify themselves from being judged worthy passengers. Likewise, we must live by faith in Christ as long as life lasts.

Jesus becomes our Lord as well as our Saviour. Our characters are by no means perfect, but they do reveal whether we have made Christ the center of our lives.

Let's tie together all this so far: God our judge wants us to be saved. His judgment is not of our worthiness, since He already knows none of us are worthy. What He must have is evidence that we believe in Jesus, our ticket to heaven. Such faith in Christ works by love (see Galatians 5:6). And "love is the fulfillment of the law" (Romans 13:10). Therefore, a life of faith in Jesus will operate in harmony with the Ten Commandments, the foundation of His will for us.

So the crucial questions in our judgment are these: Have we chosen the gift of Jesus rather than any counterfeit fulfillment? Do we trust in Christ's merits, not trying to compete with His accomplishments by attempting to create a meritorious life on our own?

It's so easy for sincere Christians to get discouraged when contemplating the judgment. They tend to admire a "supersaint" like Noble Alexander, imagining wistfully, *If I only could be like him, I'd feel more confident before a holy God.*

But first, let's remember that we all stand guilty in ourselves before God. "All of us like sheep have gone astray, each of us has turned to his own way; But the Lord has caused the iniquity of us all to fall on Him" (Isaiah 53:6, NASB).

Yes, Jesus paid it all. On the cross He offered the full price of our sin, so now we can stand clean before God.

But maybe you still feel soiled by sin. Something really serious, perhaps. You think that even if God might forgive you, you still can't forgive yourself.

Wait a minute. Who gave you the right either to forgive yourself or to condemn yourself? That is something only God, the Judge of all the earth, can do. Dare you put yourself in His place?

The apostle Paul asks, "Who will bring a charge against God's elect? God is the one who justifies; who is the one who condemns? Christ Jesus is He who died, yes, rather who was raised, who is at the right hand of God, who also intercedes for us" (Romans 8:33, 34, NASB).

So God the judge justifies you, forgives you. No human being can condemn you. You don't even have the right to condemn yourself!

Some of you may be reading this book from behind prison bars. Perhaps you're there not because of your faith in Christ, but for a crime you committed. Already you may feel bad enough, comparing yourself with a person such as Noble. Then, to make it worse, someone tells you that God only helps those who help themselves. If you get yourself into trouble, He leaves you to find your own way out of it.

How mistaken can we be? God is in the business of pulling us out of the ditches we plunge ourselves into. Isn't that what Calvary is all about? All the Lord asks is that we learn, as quickly as we can, that His way is the best way—the only truly happy way for us to live.

As we discover how to live for Him, He defends us in Heaven's judgment against the devil's accusations. And He's not only on our side up there, He's also on our side down here. As we give Him our lives day by day, He supplies us the strength to obey His will and keep His commandments.

Remember, God is the God of new beginnings: "If anyone is in Christ, he is a new creation; old things have passed away; behold, all things have become new" (2 Corinthians 5:17).

As you open your heart to Him, the Lord will bring harmony out of confusion and lead you in His unique plan for your individual life. In fact, that plan was in place even before you were born, according to Psalm 139. And no matter what mistakes you have made, God is well able to guide your life now.

Perhaps you may wonder, *How can I know what His plan is for my life?*

Proverbs 3:5, 6 declares, "Trust in the Lord with all your heart, and do not lean on your own understanding. In all your ways acknowledge Him, and He will make your paths straight" (NASB).

Notice the three conditions it outlines. First, "trust in the Lord"—live by faith in Jesus, relying on Him for all your needs. Next, "do not lean on your own understanding." In other words, recognize that God's way for you might go against your own ideas, your own wisdom. The final condition is: "In all your ways acknowledge Him," that is, accept His leadership in every aspect of your life.

When you are willing to accept these three simple conditions, God's glorious promise is yours to claim. "He will make your paths straight" (NASB). "He shall direct your paths."

Don't expect to hear a voice from heaven, or any spectacular display of God's will. He normally guides us by quietly opening doors of opportunity. If we keep our minds open to the leading of the Spirit, He reveals His will when the time is ripe.

"Wonderful," you may say. "But what if I somehow miss His signals when He tries to guide me?"

Nothing to worry about there. When we sincerely commit ourselves to God, it's His business to make His will plain to us. He will work through us, beyond us, and even in spite of us, to fulfill His purpose for our lives. And His will for us is just what we would choose for ourselves if we knew all that He does.

God leads us through His Word, often by revealing new truths for us to follow. Right now in North America, we Christians have it pretty easy compared with believers in other parts of the world. It doesn't take much courage at this point for most of us to call ourselves Christians—politicians eagerly identify with religion to help them get elected.

But what does take courage is accepting new truth revealed from the Bible. Stepping out in faith and obeying God's call through His Word.

With the freedoms we still enjoy in North America, no one is going to put us in jail for 22 years if we obey God. And nobody will arrest us if we disobey Him. The Lord Himself will not force us either way. The choice is entirely ours.

Our marvelous freedom did not come cheap. Come with me back to seventeenth-century Holland, where a group of Pilgrims have decided to start a colony in America. They are about to board the ship *Speedwell*, bound for the *Mayflower*. It's a time of excitement, but not without a sense of foreboding. They are leaving loved ones behind to cross the cold and unfamiliar Atlantic.

In their farewell hour, their beloved pastor, John Robinson, rises to speak. Listen to his words:

"Brethren, we are soon to part asunder, and the Lord only knows whether I will live to see your faces again. . . . I charge you before God to follow me no farther than I have followed Christ. If God should reveal anything to you by any other instrument of His, be as ready to receive it as you have been to receive any truth from my ministry—for I am very confident the Lord has more truth and light yet to break forth from His holy Word. . . .

"For my part, I cannot tell you how sad I am about the reformed churches. They will go no farther than the instruments of their reformation. The Lutherans cannot be drawn to go beyond what Luther saw. . . . And the Calvinists, you see, stick fast where they were left by that great man of God. . . .

"Even though these Reformers were burning and shining lights in their time, yet they did not understand all the counsel of God. But if they were living today, they would be as willing to accept further light as the light which they first received."

In his noble words we hear the true spirit of Christianity: a willingness to learn and grow, and an eagerness to walk in neglected truth that we encounter in God's Word.

Today we do not have oceans to cross or New Worlds left to discover. But new vistas of spiritual opportunity, even more exciting, may be waiting around the corner.

Suppose God offers you new truth from His Word. Are you willing to take His hand and walk in such light?

For a while you might be lonely. But the same God who stayed with Noble will also give you the strength of His presence. So why not step out in faith for the experience of your life!

If you want more:
Romans 8:28-39
Hebrews 2:14-18
Hebrews 4:14-16
Hebrews 7:25
Hebrews 8:1, 2

---

[1] Isidore Singer, ed., *The Jewish Encyclopedia* (New York: Funk and Wagnalls, 1902), Vol. II, p. 293.

[2] W. M. Chandler, *The Trial of Jesus* (New York: Empire Pub. Co., 1908), Vol. I, pp. 153, 154.

[3] See Taylor Bunch, *Behold the Man!* (Nashville: Southern Pub. Assn., 1946), pp. 64, 66. Now we understand why David in the Psalms longed to be sentenced by divine judgment: "Judge me, O Lord my God, according to thy righteousness; and let them not rejoice over me" (Psalm 35:24, KJV). Throughout the Old Testament God's people found joy in His judgment: "A father of the fatherless and a judge for the widows, is God in his holy habitation" (Psalm 68:5, KJV).

[4] Singer, p. 294.

Chapter 10

Cathy the Hostage Housewife

I'm just a slave!" Cathy, a lonely young mother, lamented to herself. Choked by routine chores, she cried, "I feel like a failure. A worthless nobody!"

Her situation resembled Linda's, whom we met in our introduction. Many women like them yearn to become something more than a house spouse. "If I could only get out into the real world," they imagine, "I'd finally be rid of my loneliness."

But no. Motherhood demands a sentence of solitary confinement within the walls of the house. Or so it seems.

Naturally, Cathy has always loved her little one, yet she craved something more than just baby talk. Not a single in-depth relationship relieved the monotony of her existence. Daytime game shows and soap operas offered familiar faces, but only counterfeit companionship.

Emotionally speaking, Cathy couldn't manage to make ends meet. She tried to cope by turning up the stereo, replaying her favorite top 40 music from high school days. But all attempts to revive her adolescent freedoms failed her.

Tony, her husband, could flee the house every morning and head off to work. She imagined him laughing and joking with his buddies at the service station. To top it off, he could leave his work behind, enjoy his supper, and turn into a couch potato for the evening. As for Cathy, you know the saying: "A woman's work is never done."

Thus she found herself tired most of the time. Burned out. But what can a 22-year-old mommy do to escape?

Sometimes Cathy wished she could just hop on a plane to Hawaii and flee from all the unfinished business that haunted her conscience. Then she felt guilty about wanting to get away. Really, she has been a good mother, all things considered.

She grew up attending parochial schools. Her childhood quest to please the Almighty took first place in her life, and she planned to consecrate herself to a religious order. In her teenage years, however, she fell in love with Tony and, abandoning her spiritual ambitions, married him. Imagining that God was displeased with her for failing to fulfill her vows, she felt guilty and quit attending church.

Soon the baby came along, and life turned into a relentless routine of changing diapers, fixing formulas, and lugging laundry baskets. The postpartum blues, which new mothers often suffer, mingled with feelings of loneliness and worthlessness to smother all hope from her heart.

Suddenly, though, sunlight from heaven penetrated the smog surrounding her. Sharon, from across the court in their apartment complex announced plans for a Bible study circle in her apartment. A half dozen young mothers from the neighborhood accepted her invitation. More for the fellowship than for spiritual food, Cathy showed up. She hoped to meet new friends. What she did not expect was the terrific time they had together with God's Word.

Sharon passed around Bibles to those who didn't have any, and introduced them to Matthew's Gospel. That first afternoon they explored chapter 1, with its list of Christ's ancestors. Cathy had struggled through those "begats" a time or two, finding them as boring as a list of names in the phone book. But her curiosity piqued when Sharon pointed out a fascinating fact of the group: among all those male "begats" in Christ's family tree, there appeared four women besides the mother of Jesus herself.

Cathy figured that such a blessed foursome must have been especially worthy saints. She listened carefully as Sharon probed one by one the background of those four female ancestors of Jesus. Three of them had made serious mistakes that would have brought disgrace upon any royal family on earth. According to Cathy's religious understanding, they should have been forced to do penance for a long while. Instead, God welcomed those women—the very ones we would be ashamed of—into heaven's royal family tree. And He went beyond that, granting them special mention there in Matthew 1 above all the other mothers in Christ's family tree.

Sharon paused thoughtfully before she posed the question "What do you think God wants to tell us here in Matthew 1?"

"I think I know," Cathy ventured. "God is telling us that He receives sinners! No matter what mistakes we might have made, He forgives us—and restores our self-respect." Then she added quietly, "You don't know how much this means to me personally."

Several of the women hugged her as she wiped away a tear. Finally Sharon commented, "Our Lord joined the fallen human race to become our Saviour. If we entrust our shattered lives to Him, He will bring harmony out of confusion and adopt us into His royal family too. Then He works within us to restore His image that was lost when sin entered the world—and every step of the way He counts us perfect in Christ."

Words can't describe the joy Cathy felt in discovering God's mercy. Nurtured by God's love in the days and weeks that followed, she found herself truly happy and fulfilled for the first time. She realized that God had never expected her to forfeit family relationships in order to live a devoted religious life. It was a joy to quit feeling guilty about being married.

God's Word became a new book to Cathy, a book of love and life. She purchased her own Bible to read every morning, selecting one of the easily understood modern translations. Each Tuesday she was always the first to arrive at Sharon's place for the study.

As the women worked their way through the book of Matthew week by week, Cathy's admiration for Christ grew more and more. She noticed how some religious leaders of His day relentlessly attacked Him with their accusations. Frequently the controversy centered on the meaning of Sabbath rest.

For example, the Pharisees had just refused Christ's gracious invitation to "Come to me, all you who are weary and burdened, and I will give you rest" (Matthew 11:28, NIV). Jesus climaxed His appeal to their hearts by proclaiming, "The Son of Man is Lord of the Sabbath" (Matthew 12:8, NIV).

"What did He mean by calling Himself 'Lord of the Sabbath'?" Cathy asked during one of the studies.

Sharon seemed eager to discuss the subject. "We've already noticed that Jesus is the Creator of the world (see John 1 and Hebrews 1). And we know He is also our Saviour. The Sabbath is heaven's appointed memorial to celebrate those twin facts of life in Christ—Creation and salvation.

"To get the full story on this," she continued, "we've got to go back to the Garden of Eden that Friday afternoon of Creation week. Jesus had just completed His work, and behold—it was very good. Then our Lord rested on the seventh day in celebration of His finished task."

Sharon proceeded to explain that Adam and Eve had done nothing to earn the right to rest, yet God invited them to share the joy of His accomplishment. By His mercy they could reap what *He* had sown.

The Sabbath rest in God's finished work symbolizes what Christianity stands for. Other world religions focus upon self-improvement, what we can do to help ourselves. But Christians celebrate God's accomplishments on our behalf. That's why the Sabbath points us away from ourselves, away from our personal works, to trust in what Jesus has done for us. Through the Sabbath we gain special insight into the meaning of Christ's sacrifice on Calvary.

It was on another Friday afternoon that Jesus finished His work for us on the cross. With His dying breath He cried, "It is finished!" His mission was accomplished and mankind redeemed. As the sun began to set, His friends laid Him to rest inside the tomb. There He remained over the Sabbath hours to memorialize His completed work for our salvation. After His quiet Sabbath repose Jesus ascended to heaven's royal throne.

"Now can you see it?" Sharon asked the group. "It's because of Christ's two great accomplishments—Creation and salvation—that He is Lord of the Sabbath. We show our faith in Him as our Maker and Redeemer by entering His Sabbath rest."

After the study ended and the other women went home, Cathy lingered behind to talk. "What does it mean for me personally to 'enter Sabbath rest'? How do I do it?"

"Well," Sharon smiled, "first you must believe that nothing more can be added to Jesus' finished work. In keeping the Sabbath, we contribute nothing of our own —we only accept God's gift of life in Christ. [1]

"Every week the Sabbath reminds us to trust Jesus for our salvation. The Bible tells us, 'Six days shalt thou labour, and do all thy work.' Yet when the sun goes down each Friday afternoon, we have to admit that our own work is never fully finished."

"I can relate to what you're saying," Cathy interjected. "It's always bothered me that I can never get to the bottom of that daily white mountain of diapers. But what does Sabbath rest have to do with dirty diapers?"

"More than we might think! God invites us to take a vacation from our work on Sabbath, to lay aside our unfinished business and rest in His completed work for us—a work that certifies our salvation."

That was a new thought to Cathy. She was silent a moment, then nodded and said, "I think I understand what you have in mind. You're saying that Sabbath rest in Christ is God's remedy for that awful unfulfilled feeling I've always struggled with—whether it is work or my salvation and relationship with God. Every week the Sabbath should remind me that God accepts me fully and freely in Jesus." She paused again. "Does that mean that I don't have to worry any more about penance or purgatory?"

Sharon smiled. "You've got it, Cathy! There's tremendous therapy for legalism in the Sabbath. The devil well knows that many who try to please God wind up trusting in their own works for salvation. The Sabbath keeps us clinging to the cross."

Cathy looked thoughtful, then continued, "I think of how I used to rummage around in my own life looking for evidence that I deserved to go to heaven. Now, week by week the Sabbath assures me that despite my shortcomings I stand complete in Christ.

"Hey, that's great! Why, it's just beautiful. But wait a minute—doesn't the New Testament change the day of worship from the seventh to the first day of the week?"

"Let's check that out," her friend offered. "Surprisingly, only eight New Testament texts even mention what we call Sunday. The first six record the simple fact that Christ arose and appeared to His disciples on the first day of the week." [2]

"What about the other two texts? I really want to get to the bottom of this."

"Acts 20:7 mentions a meeting on the dark part of the first day of the week. Actually, though, this was Saturday night, as a number of versions point out. The disciples broke bread, which they sometimes did every day (see Acts 2:46). Now let's see that last text about Sunday." She flipped through the Bible. "Here it is [1 Corinthians 16:2]: 'On the first day of the week let each one of you lay something aside, storing up as he may prosper, that there be no collections when I come' [NKJV]."

"That sounds like a worship service to me."

"Look closer," Sharon urged. "Is Paul really taking up a collection at church on the first day of the week? Notice those words 'lay something aside, storing up.' You see, this text doesn't involve a worship meeting. It's about putting aside money on the first day of the week so the believers would have something saved up to give Paul when he came to visit."

"That makes sense," Cathy concluded. She thought a moment. "I guess it looks like there's no Bible support whatever for worshiping on the first day of the week. That would mean that Sunday just isn't scriptural! But—how do we know today's Saturday is still the Bible Sabbath?"

"Well, we know Jesus died on the sixth day of the week, the day we call 'Good Friday.' And Christ rose on the first day of the week, honored as Easter Sunday. Now, what was the day in between the death of Christ on Friday and His resurrection on Sunday?"

"The seventh day."

"Of course. The Bible calls this day between our Good Friday and Resurrection Sunday 'the sabbath day according to the commandment' [Luke 23:56]."

"That's our Saturday, all right," Cathy concurred. "No question about it."

"And here's something else you'll be interested in. In more than 100 languages spoken today, the word for their seventh day of the week is the word for Sabbath. For example, *Sabado* is the Spanish word for the seventh day of the week. You don't have to be Hispanic to recognize that it means 'Sabbath.' In Russian, I understand that the word for the seventh day is also the translation of Sabbath. Many languages all over the world confirm that our seventh day is really God's Sabbath."

Cathy listened with deep interest to everything Sharon said. Then she leaned back with a sigh. "All this seems incredible—yet it makes sense just the same. I guess my last question is Why don't more Christians keep the Sabbath?"

"Well, more and more are discovering Sabbath rest. Every week around the world more than 7,000 believers are keeping their first Sabbath in Seventh-day Adventist churches."

"Maybe I should be one of them," Cathy said with a teasing smile.

"If you want, I'll be happy to pick you up for church," Sharon offered. "You'll love our church family."

"But I always do my laundry on Saturday," she replied with surprise.

"Why not another day? Your washing machine won't know the difference!"

"You've got all the answers, don't you?" Cathy laughed. Then she sobered. "That raises a lot of questions—like about my husband. Tony won't want me to leave him alone in the house on Saturdays. He works all week and likes me home then."

"I faced the same problem with my husband at first. I just had to try to explain to him and hope he would understand. He does now."

Cathy took a deep breath. "You know, I really want to obey God's will . . ."

"I've got an idea!" Sharon broke in. "Tell Tony that you're going to church to learn how to be a better wife. He'll relate to that! Besides, you still have Sunday mornings together with him, don't you?"

That night Cathy discussed with her husband her thoughts about attending church that Sabbath. Sure enough, he wasn't exactly thrilled with the idea. So she reminded him, "You go off fishing on Saturdays whenever you want to—why can't I go to church?"

What could he say?

It took some commitment for Cathy to change her religious lifestyle, to begin observing the biblical concept of the Sabbath. She recalled hearing about what it cost the early Christians to live for Jesus. They could have saved themselves from being fed to the lions by simply offering a pinch of incense to the emperor in pagan worship. That was their test of their devotion to Him.

What about our test today? Here in our land of freedom it usually involves no risk to declare ourselves Christians. Politicians actually find it useful to wear His name like a bumper sticker. But to actually live for Jesus takes courage. "This is love for God: to obey His commands" (1 John 5:3, NIV).

Talk is cheap. Genuine faith in Jesus, however, loves Him enough to accept Him as Lord of the Sabbath. Do we consider what He has done for us as our Creator and Saviour important enough to lay aside our own works and enter His rest? You can see how the Sabbath tests our faith in Christ and our love for Him.

Cathy never regretted her decision to observe the Sabbath. At first it seemed strange to disrupt her weekend plans, but now she wouldn't have it any other way. She has met many new friends who share her faith.

Surprisingly, Tony seems to be warming up to her new church family. The church members had a picnic and softball game the other Sunday, and he had a great time. He has even mentioned once or twice that he might check out the services one Sabbath.

Did you know that through all eternity the Sabbath will unite us for worship as one big family of God?

" 'As the new heavens and the new earth that I make will endure before me,' declares the Lord, 'so will your name and descendants endure. From one New Moon to another and from one Sabbath to another, all mankind will come and bow down before me,' says the Lord" (Isaiah 66:22, 23, NIV).

Great news, wouldn't you say? Forever we will keep our personal identity—and our descendants, our children. We will enjoy heaven with our families! And all of us together will worship our Lord on His Sabbath day.

Try to imagine that first wonderful Sabbath together with Jesus. Picture Him leading the worship service, then taking a stroll with us along the river of life.

I can hardly wait, can you?

But think about it. If we are going to worship together on God's holy Sabbath throughout the ceaseless ages of eternity, why not begin right now?

If you want more:
> Genesis 2:1-3
> Isaiah 58:13, 14
> Ezekiel 20:12, 20
> Hebrews 4:1-11
> Revelation 14:12

---

[1] The word *Sabbath* means "a cessation," finished activity. And the Hebrew root of *Sabbath* is translated "to bring to an end," or "to cease," representing something finished so completely nothing need be added (see Daniel 9:27; Isaiah 13:11; Psalm

46:9). Thus the Sabbath honors the finished work of God in which we rest—work done so well it can't be improved upon.

[2] Matthew 28:1; Mark 16:2, 9; Luke 24:1; John 20:1, 19.

[3] If you want to know more about Sabbath rest in Jesus, I know of a book that will probably clear up any question you have: *When God Made Rest*, by George Vandeman. Just drop me a note, and I'll be glad to get you a copy.

Chapter 11

Benjamin's New Knife

Young Benjamin grabbed a knife and lunged toward a teasing playmate. By something of a miracle the boy survived the attack. And a greater miracle of God's mercy transformed Benjamin's knife of potential death into the knife of life he now wields as a world-renowned brain surgeon.

Dr. Benjamin Carson didn't grow up on easy street there in Detroit's inner city. His mother raised him by herself, working three jobs. Every day she prayed with Benjamin and his brother, and on Sabbaths she took them to church.

Benjamin loved the stories about Jesus and His healings. And when he heard in Sabbath school about mission doctors helping people in far-off lands, then and there he dedicated his life to become a physician.

Walking home along the glass-strewn sidewalks, Benjamin shared his dream with his mother. She offered both encouragement and counsel. "Benny, if you ask the Lord for something, believing He will do it, then He will help you. But you've got to do your part by bringing up those bad marks in school. You'll never become a doctor if all you do is watch television."

And so a wise mother nurtured in her son a love for books that catapulted him from the bottom of his class to the top. Benjamin won a scholarship to Yale University and then to the University of Michigan Medical School. At the age of 33 he became director of pediatric neurosurgery at Baltimore's famed Johns Hopkins University School of Medicine.

You may have heard Dr. Carson's name on the news. In September 1987, he was the primary surgeon in a dramatic 22-hour operation separating a pair of Siamese twins joined at the back of the head. *Time* magazine called it "an operation of staggering complexity." *Newsweek* said it "could quite possibly be the most complex surgical procedure performed in this century."

Dr. Carson first earned national headlines in 1985 for performing the delicate surgery known as hemispherectomy, the surgical removal of half of the upper part of the brain. As a boy, Benjamin showed little potential of performing such feats as a highly skilled servant of humanity. Along with the typical obstacles to success faced by any youth of his race, Benjamin had a violent temper. Without a moment's notice he would attack with a rock, hammer, or anything else at hand. Even a knife.

His temper problem climaxed at the age of 14. "A boy had done something very minor," Dr. Carson recalls, "and I grabbed a knife and tried to stab him. Thank God, the steel blade snapped harmlessly as it struck the playmate's heavy belt buckle."

Benjamin fled the scene in horror, shocked that he had almost killed a fellow human being. He ran home, then into the bathroom and shut the door. Trembling, he knelt and gave his heart to the Lord once and for all. You may have read Dr. Carson's incredible story in a number of national publications, including *Guidepost, Ebony,* and *Message* magazines.

Of all the professions, none exacts more vigorous demands than neurosurgery. Dr. Carson must manage his time with wisdom and utmost efficiency. That's why he opens each day with two hours of prayer and Bible study. He knows by experience the truth of Christ's saying, "Seek first the kingdom of God and His righteousness, and all these things shall be added to you" (Matthew 6:33).

Dr. Carson says, "If I don't want a Christian experience that's 'for the birds,' then I had better get up with the birds to seek the Lord early every morning."

Prayer is great time management. First, it keeps us focused on what's most important in life. Experts agree that the foundation of managing our time is setting goals and priorities—then sticking with them. But it's so easy to become disoriented and distracted—like the farmer who rose early to plow his "south forty."

First he needed to oil the old tractor, but he ran out of oil, so he went to the shop to fetch some more. On the way he noticed that the pigs weren't fed. He turned aside to the corncrib, where he found some sacks. That reminded him that the potatoes were sprouting, so he started for the potato pit. Passing the woodpile, he remembered that his wife wanted fuel for the stove. As he bent down for some sticks, an ailing chicken limped by. He dropped the wood and reached for the sick bird. When evening came, the poor fellow still had not gotten his tractor to the field.

Obviously being busy isn't enough. We must organize our lives according to what is most essential and live accordingly.

How do we know what's most important? Step back and survey the big picture. What means the most to you? What will last in the long run?

Most of us live in violation of our own values. Surveys insist that health and family values are more important to us than wealth or career. Yet we bury ourselves in our work, ignoring our loved ones—as well as our own need for being refreshed. Those few who manage to make it to the top often ruin their lives getting there.

Pollsters also tell us that Americans rank spiritual values high on their priorities. Somehow, though, our relationship with God gets buried amid the rat race.

Prayer prevents us from cheating ourselves out of that which means the most to us. Putting first things first with God every morning helps us stay on track all day long.

Have you gotten sidetracked? Let's take stock and rank our priorities in order of importance:

A—Absolute essentials: preserving our relationship with God and our families, guarding our health, and earning a living.

B—Beneficial activities: wholesome reading and educational television, along with recreation. (That's re-creation, not wreck-reation.)

C—Cravings we have for harmless fun, such as innocent TV programs.

Through prayer Dr. Carson manages to preserve his priorities. He may not have much leisure for categories B and C, but he certainly looks after his main agenda, category A. He knows the occupational stress that neurosurgeons suffer threatens their homelife. Many of their marriages fail. But the Carsons have managed not just to survive but to thrive together.

Benjamin treasures his wife, Candy, whom he met at Yale, where she was a music major. He is an affectionate father to his three little boys: Murray, Ben, Jr., and Rhoeyce. You can be sure they are glad to have a praying father. How much we all need prayer to help keep priorities in order!

Another principle of time management is to work with energy and enthusiasm. We can't accomplish much when burdened with worry, jealousy, guilt, or discouragement. They sap our energies and cripple our performance.

In prayer we lay our burdens to rest. Dr. Carson has learned that "the peace of God, which surpasses all understanding, will guard your hearts and minds through Christ Jesus" (Philippians 4:7). Fellowship with God relieves and refreshes him, strengthening him to endure those long and lonely hours at the operating table. We could all accomplish more good in less time through Christ, who gives us strength in prayer.

Yet another key to time management is working well with others. How much time we waste at war with each other! Petty politics at the office. Lawsuits against neighbors. Misunderstandings with in-laws. Battles with loved ones at home.

Prayer brings peace. Through prayer God humbles us and comforts us so that we become loving and forgiving, thus smoothing our relationships. Hearts melt and enemies become friends.

Human lives depend upon how well Dr. Carson can function with his medical staff. Walking the tightrope between life and death creates intense pressures that strain relationships. Benjamin manages through prayer to retain his compassion and good humor, which contributes greatly to his staff's effectiveness.

I think you can see why prayer helps us live productively and efficiently. Dr. Carson has another secret of time management, something that also relates to his relationship with Jesus—the Sabbath. For all the reasons prayer enhances time management, so does the Sabbath.

Each week God's holy day reaffirms our priorities. On Friday afternoon, as the sun sets, the last thing we may want is to stop whatever we are doing and enter Christ's rest. And so the Sabbath brings us a weekly test of what is most important to us. Will we consider what Jesus has done for us worth more than what the world offers—enough to set aside its business and pleasure, its news and sports and shopping? Will we take the day off as a spiritual vacation to be with our families and fellow believers?

It's not always easy to lay aside life's duties for the Sabbath. But any time you take a vacation, you've got to make arrangements with your employer, your friends, and family—and the Sabbath is our weekly spiritual vacation.

Yes, it takes some inconvenience and perhaps even hardship to keep that appointment with God. But Sabbath rest leaves us refreshed and rejuvenated. When we "come apart, . . . and rest a while" every Sabbath, the energy we receive makes for wonderful time management in conquering the challenges of the new week.

The Sabbath also enhances relationships within the family and friendship circle. All week long people race past each other, out of time and out of touch, creating superficial relationships. Sabbath rest makes it possible to restore and deepen those precious ties that should bind our hearts together. This again is good for time management, not to mention improving our quality of life.

Just ask the Carson family. When the sun sets Friday evening, they gather for stories and songs. The next morning they go to church together for worship and fellowship. Following a thoroughly enjoyable dinner, often with friends, they like to spend Sabbath afternoons in nature.

Medical emergencies may call Dr. Carson back to the hospital, and he considers any such act of compassion perfectly suited for the Sabbath. Normally, though, he can arrange for associates to cover for him so he can have his Sabbaths off. It's important to him to spend God's special day with the ones he loves most.

Do you see the potential in Sabbath rest for enriching every part of our lives all week long? And observing the Sabbath is indeed effective time management. But its greatest value is that Jesus is the Lord of the Sabbath. The Bible says it represents the special sign between Him and His people. A sign that He sets us apart from the world to be His children (Ezekiel 20:12). And He invites us to respond in turn: "Hallow my sabbaths" (verse 20). That is, "set the seventh day apart for Me, just as I have set it apart for you. Let's spend that time together each week."

Since the Sabbath offers such blessings, why has most of the Christian world forgotten it? To answer that question, we must go back to the early centuries of the Christian era. Believers, though ready to sacrifice life itself rather than yield their faith in Christ, still somehow allowed pagan influences to corrupt that faith. They adopted false teachings that suffocated pure gospel truth.

Quietly and gradually the apostasy spread. Although many believers refused to compromise the gospel, the church in general suffered a serious loss of faith.

Should this surprise us? After all, had not God's people throughout history continually wandered from His will?

The New Testament had even predicted problems within the church. Peter the apostle warned, "There will be false teachers among you, who will secretly bring in destructive heresies. . . . And many will follow their destructive ways" (2 Peter 2:1, 2). Paul also prophesied that truth would suffer (see Acts 20:29, 30).

Just how did the church lose sight of Sabbath rest in Christ? Soon after the apostles died, drastic changes transformed Christianity. We see this in the life and teachings of the church fathers. Consider Origen, for example, a respected and eloquent defender of Christianity in the early centuries. He taught that "perfect" saints, or those nearly so, enjoyed special access to God. But so-called simple believers had to content themselves with lesser blessings. Those who seemed closest to perfection became objects of veneration. People coveted their prayers as if they had a hotline to God through their superior piety.

Of course, such teaching is foreign to the gospel, which makes every Christian equally accepted in Christ. Yet all manner of rites and ceremonies that Christ and the apostles had never heard of infiltrated the church. Around the third century, the concept of penance entered to help confessing Christians take sin seriously. Unfortuntely, it also prevented repenting sinners from rejoicing in sins forgiven and having the assurance of complete acceptance with God.

Then in the early fifth century Simeon Stylites climbed to the top of a tall pillar and made his home there. He determined to live quite literally above the world, safe beyond the reach of its comforts and pleasures. For several decades he remained perched on a small platform atop various pillars, exposed and unsheltered from the weather. Finally death gave him rest from his works.

Most of the Christian church venerated Simeon Stylites as a spiritual hero. Upon his death the cities of Antioch and Constantinople competed for the possession of his body. For six centuries ascetics known as pillar saints followed his example by living up on pillars away from the world, pursuing their personal perfection.

Not surprisingly, amid such a concentration on personal spiritual behavior, Sabbath rest—with its recognition of dependence on God—fell into disfavor. In its place rose the celebration of Sunday, the first day of the week.

How did this come about? We have seen one factor in the church's growing absorption in perfecting the spiritual life through certain ascetic practices that unfortunately led to a form of legalism. Now let's look at still another one. It will take us on a fascinating tour through early Christian history.

The first-century church members wanted to distance themselves from anything Jewish. The Jews, you see, had put themselves in the emperor's disfavor by constantly revolting to regain national independence. And Rome had struck back. In A.D. 70 its armies stormed Jerusalem, starving, burning, crucifying, or otherwise killing a quarter million Jews. Numerous anti-Jewish riots swept the empire, climaxed by even stiffer penalties for Jews.

Because Christians and Jews shared the same heritage, Romans tended to treat both groups the same. The Christians naturally thought this was unfair. They wanted peace with the emperor, rendering to Caesar his due. Yet they suffered just as if they were rebellious Jews—on top of the persecution already theirs for Jesus' sake.

After the second destruction of Jerusalem in the year 135, Emperor Hadrian outlawed Jewish worship—especially Sabbathkeeping. Christians felt compelled to divorce themselves completely from their Hebrew heritage. Gradually they welcomed customs and holy days from the pagan Roman Empire, including its weekly day of sun worship.

For several centuries Christians observed both the Sabbath and Sunday, with the first day of the week quickly gaining more and more prominence. This side-by-side practice continued into the sixth century, with the true Sabbath still holding firm in many areas. But finally Sunday completely eclipsed the Sabbath throughout the empire, although even then pockets of Sabbathkeepers remained here and there.

The Epistle of Barnabas, written around the year 135, contains the first explicit reference to Sunday observance. It is interesting to notice the case presented there for abandoning the Sabbath.

Barnabas argues that Sabbathkeeping is impossible. Impossible until the future life in eternity, because in the present world all believers are impure and unholy. The writer asks, How can we have rest until God's work within our hearts is complete? But in heaven, he states, "we shall be able to treat it [the Sabbath] as holy, after we have first been made holy ourselves." [1]

To Barnabas, holiness meant perfection of character. But in the New Testament, being a saint means deciding to repent of sin, being set apart to live for God.

Apparently the church was forgetting the gospel through misunderstanding Sabbath rest. We don't rest in Christ because of our character development, but rather because of His accomplishments—what He has done. The apostle Paul taught that God "has made us accepted in the Beloved" (Ephesians 1:6). "You are complete in Him" (Colossians 2:10). This is the message of the Sabbath.

Had the early Christians continued to grasp clearly that salvation was God's accomplishment, not theirs, they never would have forsaken Sabbath rest. Let's explore this further to learn how legalism, or man's obsession with attaining perfection, assisted Sunday in overtaking the Sabbath.

For Christians in the mid-second century, the main reason argued for observing Sunday as worship was that God began to create our world on the first day of the week, when God made light. Before long, Christ's resurrection on Sunday became the dominant support for Sunday sacredness. Later on, another reason gained prominence—the fact that the Holy Spirit came to the church on Pentecost Sunday. *The Convert's Catechism of Catholic Doctrine,* 1977 edition, documents this: "The Church substituted Sunday for Saturday, because Christ rose from the dead on a Sunday, and the Holy Ghost descended upon the apostles on a Sunday." [2]

A favorite verse quoted by Church Fathers in establishing Sunday sacredness was Malachi 4:2: "But to you who fear My name the Sun of Righteousness shall arise with healing in His wings." Sunday symbolized spiritual "healing" within the human heart because Christians considered

Jesus as the Sun of righteousness. The process of spiritual healing begins when God brings sinners light. Then comes conversion—new life in Christ through His resurrection. Finally the Holy Spirit of Pentecost lives within the believer, restoring the image of God.

All these elements of spiritual renewal exist because of events that happened on the first day of the week. One author summarized it this way: "For the Sunday assembly . . . [is] a celebration of the re-creation of men." Thus many have regarded it as a memorial of God's power to re-create human hearts through the new birth and keep us from sinning.

Well, what could be wrong with that?

First, you must remember that we are dealing with something subtle here. A sincere error, perhaps, but an error just the same. Something appearing as gospel truth but secretly destroying faith.

Let's go back to Simeon Stylites for a moment, and the problem with Sunday sacredness will come into focus. What was Stylites doing on top of that pillar, high in the air? Pursuing sinlessness, spiritual renewal.

As a youth, Stylites had shown unusual religious fervor. While still a shepherd boy in his early teens, he entered a monastery and dedicated himself to imitating the example of Christ. Before long, his quest for Christlikeness took him into absolute solitude. There he passed the entire Lenten season without eating or drinking, seeking to subdue the flesh so that the Spirit could rule in his life.

Not satisfied with his spiritual progress, Stylites disciplined himself to stand upright for long periods of time. Finally in the year 433 he mounted a nine-foot pillar in order to escape the world. His pillars got taller and taller as he imagined himself getting closer and closer to God. Eventually, though, he died atop a pillar 60 feet high, never having realized perfection.

Five stories up in the air is pretty high, but not high enough to match the spiritual accomplishments of Jesus. If Simeon Stylites had understood Sabbath rest, he wouldn't have climbed that pillar in the first place. Instead, he would have accepted Christ's perfection as his own accomplishment.

Are you beginning to see what's wrong with Sunday sacredness? It focuses attention on the holiness of the Christian—an imperfect, incomplete ground of hope. The Sabbath, on the other hand, honors the perfect work of Christ already done for us—work pronounced by God to be "very good," done so well that it's finished forever, and—nothing more can be added to improve it.

Certainly Christian growth is important. But we cannot confuse what the Bible calls the "fruit" of the gospel—a changed life—with the gospel itself. The gospel, you recall, is the doing and dying of Christ. The fruit of the gospel is a transformed life because of the indwelling Christ. Do you see the difference?

The Sabbath memorializes the gospel, the finished work of Christ in His life and death. The early Christians came to regard Sunday as memorializing the fruit of the gospel, the unfinished work of Christ in our lives. The difference between the two is crucial. Only Sabbath rest gives us that blessed assurance that all is well with our souls.

By turning away from Sabbath rest in the completed work of Christ, the church broke the very heart of Christianity. Satan diverted attention from the cross, focusing instead on the imperfect spiritual experience of believers.

And remember, Sundaykeeping has no support in the New Testament. Jesus said, "For the Son of Man is Lord even of the Sabbath" (Matthew 12:8).

By now you may be wondering, What difference does it make, this Sabbath-Sunday business? None at all, unless we have committed our lives to Jesus Christ. Since He is Lord of the Sabbath, faith in Him involves entering that rest in His completed salvation.

No wonder many millions of sincere Christians the world over are making plans for worship and fellowship this coming Sabbath. Why not be among them? You already love the Lord—this is just one more step with Jesus.

Often we hear the words "Expect a miracle!" Usually the idea is to get what we want from God. But God has a better plan—expect a miracle in getting what He wants. When we step forward by faith to obey Him, He will indeed work miracles for us, if that's what it requires.

Our Saviour's gracious promise is worth whatever trouble it takes to accept it: "Come to Me, all who are weary and heavy laden, and I will give you rest" (Matthew. 11:28, NASB).

If you want more:
> Exodus 20:8-11
> Isaiah 58:13, 14
> Hebrews 4:1-11
> Hebrews 8:10
> 1 John 2:3, 4

---

[1] Translation by E. Goodspeed, pp. 40, 41, quoted in Samuele Bacchiocchi, *From Sabbath to Sunday*, p. 221.

[2] Peter Geiermann, *The Convert's Catechism of Catholic Doctrine* (Rockford, Ill: Tan Books, 1977), p. 50.

Chapter 12

Larry's
Mid-life Crisis

Let me introduce you to Larry, a 43-year-old attorney. Last summer, for no apparent reason, he began feeling dissatisfied with life, yearning for better things. Not anything financial—already he enjoyed this world's comforts and pleasures.

So why his mysterious restlessness? Larry felt unfulfilled and incomplete, even though he was a decent, hardworking citizen. Exactly what it was that he wanted or needed to feel good about himself again, he just didn't know.

Back in 1968 Larry had entered law school determined to make a difference in the world, to champion the cause of civil rights. [1]

Early in his career as a lawyer he championed the poor and oppressed. Unfortunately, as his family grew, the financial demands upon him also increased. Thus he felt forced to abandon social activism and pursue something more lucrative, personal-injury law.

Larry excelled in his new specialty and eventually enjoyed a luxurious income. His goal at first had been to provide a decent life for his loved ones. Before he realized it, however, he became mired in materialism—the very lifestyle he had condemned back in the sixties.

With self-doubt swirling inside him, Larry began rethinking his priorities. Was he fulfilling his purpose in life?

Or had he become just another businessman, out to make a buck like everyone around him?

He was a man in mid-life crisis. Psychologist Gary Collins describes the phenomenon: "Beginning in the late 30s or early 40s, it is a period of life characterized by self-examination, reevaluation of beliefs and values, readjustment to physical change and reconsideration of one's lifestyle and priorities." [2] I suppose you could say that men in mid-life crisis are having second thoughts about nearly everything. Maybe such self-evaluation is a good idea. Could it be God's way of waking us up and straightening us out before life has passed us by?

The more Larry pondered his circumstances, the more he despaired about the future. He concluded that he could never even begin to solve the social injustice around him. Coming to terms with the failed dreams of his youth was downright depressing. His sense of self-worth plummeted.

Low self-esteem is a common element of mid-life crisis. In fact, it afflicts people of all age groups. Surveys insist that nine out of ten of us suffer from some sense of inferiority.

You know how it goes. A student in law school judges himself inferior to the graduate who just passed his bar exam. This new lawyer envies an already prosperous attorney—who in turn feels less valuable than the mayor of the city. Now, the mayor considers himself unimportant compared with the governor. And the governor—well, he wishes he were president of the United States.

Our nation's leader enthroned in the White House is immune to inferiority, we might imagine. Not really! In comparing himself with great leaders of the past like Lincoln and Washington, even the president may feel pangs of low self-esteem.

The whole business of self-worth seems to be a no-win situation. There's always someone around or in memory more successful, more intelligent, more popular.

Larry observed also that whatever limited success we do achieve may not last once it is earned. Today's hero can be tomorrow's castaway. The ballplayer who delights the cheering crowd with a go-ahead home run will forfeit his popularity immediately through a game-losing error.

Our world's value system of wealth, power, good looks, and success provides no security. Even so, we insist upon measuring one another and ourselves by the possession of such so-called qualities as: "He's worth $10 million." "Isn't she a doll?" "Another promotion!"

The Bible emphasizes an entirely different set of values, wherein we find the key to genuine self-esteem. Knowing what we're worth and why we are important provides an entirely new outlook on life.

We ought to pay attention to what God says about self-worth and human value. After all, He created us in the first place. Then, after sin severed our relationship with Him, He sacrificed His life to save us. In that ultimate price He paid for us at Calvary we can tell how much we are worth:

"For God so loved the world that he gave his one and only Son, that whoever believes in him shall not perish but have eternal life" (John 3:16).[3]

God exchanged the life of His Son to ransom a lost world. In fact, Jesus would have died just for you, or for me. The apostle Paul said, "I live by faith in the Son of God, who loved *me* and gave himself for *me*" (Galatians 2:20). It's one thing to believe that Jesus died for the whole world, but it's especially wonderful to realize that He died for me personally, and for you. That's how precious each one of us is in God's sight.

Christ traded His life for ours! Our heavenly Father considers each one of us equal in value to His Son Jesus. It seems incredible, but Christ Himself recognized this when He prayed for His disciples, "You . . . have loved them even as [as much as] you have loved me" (John 17:23).

When Larry first learned this, he couldn't believe it. How could God consider him so valuable, sinful as he was?

Jack, Larry's Christian law partner, explained that our importance to God does not rest upon our spiritual accomplishments. If that were true, God could have no relation-ship with us, for "all have sinned and fall short of the glory of God" (Romans 3:23).

Think about it. When a car crashes, wrapping itself around a tree, it loses its value. Not so with human beings. When the human race wrecked at the tree in the Garden of Eden and became defiled by sin, we remained every bit as valuable to God. Doomed to certain death, but precious just the same.

Where's the proof of this? "God demonstrates his own love for us in this: While we were yet sinners, Christ died for us" (Romans 5:8). God loves us as much as He loves Jesus! As long as we keep this in mind, is it possible to feel inferior at all to anyone, anywhere?

In His love the Lord adopts us through Christ into His royal family: "How great is the love the Father has lavished on us, that we should be called children of God! And that is what we are!" (1 John 3:1).

Eventually Larry couldn't hold himself back from re-sponding to such love. He decided to repent of his sins and trust in Jesus. Thrilled with his new experience, he ex-claimed to his friend Jack, "Just think! From a hostage of the devil to a child of God."

His law partner explained to him how God certifies our royal adoption by giving us His Holy Spirit: "Because you are sons, God sent the Spirit of his Son into our hearts, the Spirit who calls out, 'Abba, Father' " (Galatians 4:6).

Notice that Paul calls the Holy Spirit "the Spirit of his Son," because He comes to us through Jesus. The Bible speaks of three persons in the "Godhead"—the Father, the Son, and the Holy Spirit (compare Colossians 2:9 and Matthew 28:19). In a mysterious and wonderful way the presence of the Spirit brings to every Christian both Jesus and the Father: "We will come to him, and make our home with him" (John 14:23).

Christ gave His promise to the disciples during His last night with them before Calvary. Noticing their sad faces, He assured them, "I will not leave you as orphans; I will come to you" (verse 18). It is through the Holy Spirit that Jesus lives with us. He told the disciples that now He would be especially close to them (John 16:7). You see, by the Spirit He actually lives within our hearts, our minds.

Obviously, our minds are too limited to understand everything about God and how He lives within us by His Spirit. That should not bother us, though, because the world is full of things that we humans can't explain—yet we accept them as fact. Take electricity, for example. Much about it remains a mystery, nevertheless we welcome its help for daily living. Likewise with our heavenly friend, the Holy Spirit.

Just think—the living, loving God takes up residence within our hearts! Of course the privilege of being God's child, of having His indwelling Spirit, carries some responsibilities. Notice, for example, a passage such as the following: "Do you not know that your body is a temple of the Holy Spirit, who is in you, whom you have received from God? You are not your own; you were bought at a price. Therefore honor God with your body" (1 Corinthians 6:19, 20).

Larry thought this seemed reasonable enough. If God makes our human body His temple, the least we can do is take care of it. Determined to give more attention to good health, he began walking several miles every day for exercise, and he's been taking regular time off for relaxing with his family. He also exchanged his fast food lunches for the more wholesome salad bar fare.

Smoking never had been a problem for Larry. It didn't make sense to him, burning up one's health and wallet for a habit offering nothing in return but polluted air for everyone around. No, Marlboro Country with its over-crowded cemetery never had much attraction for him.

However, he had fallen into the trap of occasional drinking. With life becoming less and less meaningful, he had tried to fill the emptiness with alcohol whenever he began feeling depressed. One day at lunch he brought up the subject with Jack.

"I've known you for two years now, and I've never seen you order a drink. Your way makes sense, I admit, but I still don't see anything wrong with a glass of wine now and then. Doesn't it help digestion?"

Jack smiled. "I think there are better ways to keep your stomach from growling, like cutting down on that salad dressing. Look, Larry, you know the problems of alcohol abuse in our society. Addiction sneaks up on you—in a time of crisis, people find themselves depending more upon alcohol, and afterward they may have trouble cutting down again. They're hooked.

"In fact," Jack continued, "I've been worried about you lately concerning this very thing."

Larry knew the truth of what his friend was saying. His alcohol consumption had been creeping upward.

Jack waited a moment, then pressed on. "Besides all this, in Bible times if a person became drunk, he maybe fell off his donkey. These days, someone drunk is likely to cause a fatal accident. [4] How many of our personal-injury cases have their roots in someone getting out of control through alcohol?"

"You're right," Larry replied solemnly. "I used to think that a glass of wine was soothing for the nerves—good medicine. But I suppose we have medications now that don't have the dangerous side effects of alcohol."

Jack took advantage of that comment to introduce an important spiritual truth. "The Bible offers us a wonderful substitute for alcohol: 'Do not get drunk on wine, which leads to debauchery. Instead, be filled with the Spirit' [Ephesians 5:18]."

"I like that, but how do I go about getting filled with the Spirit?"

"It's really simple," Jack replied. "Jesus said, 'The words I have spoken to you are spirit and they are life' [John 6:63]. So it's through reading God's Word day by day that we receive the filling of the Holy Spirit."

Thus Larry began faithfully taking time for prayer and study every morning. Often the Lord reveals areas of his life that need correction. Such adjustments may be painful sometimes, but he considers the privilege of being filled with the Holy Spirit well worth the effort to surrender.

Character development is the work of a lifetime. But —thank God—each day as we yield our lives to Him while trusting in Jesus as our Saviour, our names remain in heaven's book of life. And the Holy Spirit lives within us to warm our hearts and give us strength. Here is the real and only solution to emptiness and loneliness!

There's another exciting dimension to Christian living besides our personal relationship with God. He not only unites us to Himself through the Holy Spirit, but He also joins us to each other. The Bible says that "in Christ we [Christians] who are many form one body, and each member belongs to all the others" (Romans 12:5).

Together we form one body of believers with Christ as our head. So we are even closer than brothers and sisters —we actually share the same body of Jesus! The Holy Spirit lives within us all and knits our hearts together in Christ.

As individual members of Christ's body, we each have our important place: "Now the body is not made up of one part but of many. If the foot should say, 'Because I am not a hand, I do not belong to the body,' it would not for that reason cease to be part of the body. And if the ear should say, 'Because I am not an eye, I do not belong to the body,' it would not for that reason cease to be part of the body. If the whole body were an eye, where would the sense of hearing be? If the whole body were an ear, where would the sense of smell be? But in fact God has arranged the parts in the body, every one of them, just as He wanted them to be" (1 Corinthians 12:14-18).

So even as the different members of our physical bodies have varying functions on behalf of the whole, each Christian has special responsibilities to fellow members in the body of Christ.

"If a man's gift is prophesying, let him use it in proportion to his faith. If it is serving, let him serve; if it is teaching, let him teach; if it is encouraging, let him encourage; if it is contributing to the needs of others, let him give earnestly; if it is leadership, let him govern diligently; if it is showing mercy, let him do it cheerfully" (Romans 12:6-8).

Not everyone has the same spiritual gift. Many Christians today don't understand that. For example, they may think that all believers must have the same gift of tongues. But that isn't so. The Bible says, "There are different kinds of gifts, but the same Spirit. There are different kinds of service, but the same Lord" (1 Corinthians 12:4, 5). (One lesson from the tragic downfall of Jimmy Swaggart and Jim Bakker is that speaking in tongues is no evidence that God is leading in one's life. Furthermore, Jesus warned of counterfeit spiritual gifts—see Matthew 7:20-23.)

Larry took an inventory exam and discovered what his spiritual gifts are.[5] He concluded that since God had especially blessed him financially, he had a responsibility to use that spiritual gift to "contribute to the needs of others." Also, with his expertise in law he could volunteer some time to serve needy clients.

By using his spiritual gifts, he has rediscovered the dream of his youth—the dream of making a difference in our world of need. He finds more fulfillment from his service for Christ than he does from his professional law practice.

An unexpected benefit has come from his new life of sharing. Helping others spiritually makes Larry hunger for a deeper spiritual experience himself. Just as someone who exercises feels the need for more food, Larry, by using his spiritual gifts, craves for more of Jesus, the Bread of life.

He asked Jack for advice about how to deepen his relationship with Christ. His friend recommended a biography on the life of Jesus, *The Desire of Ages,* a beloved classic from the turn of the century.[6]

Larry learned from Christ's unselfish example the importance of reaching out to those in need. He used to think he could keep religion to himself, boycotting church services while worshiping God alone under the big tree in his backyard. Now he understands the responsibilities and privileges of being a believer. Fellow members of Christ's body need him, and he needs them.

People of the world use God's gifts of wealth and influence to enrich themselves at the expense of those less fortunate. But in the body of Christ, any advantage we may have over someone else—be it educational, financial, having special talents, or anything else—every advantage makes us the servant of those who lack what we have.

Larry welcomes every Christian he meets into friendship as a fellow member of Christ's body—closer even than his natural brother and sister. And those who are not Christians he regards as candidates for the kingdom of God.

Larry has been attending worship services every week. He has more friends now—people who really love him—than he ever thought possible.

Thanks to the Holy Spirit in his own heart, he has discovered the truth of what William Arthur Ward once said: "The surest cure for loneliness, the quickest way to happiness, is found in this, a simple creed: Go serve someone in greater need."

If you want more:
  John 14
  John 15
  John 16
  Romans 8:12-27
  1 Peter 4:10, 11

---

[1] In this chapter I have taken unusual liberties with the story in order to illustrate various important points.

[2] Gary R. Collins, *Christian Counseling* (Waco, Tex.: Word Books, 1980), p. 251.

[3] Bible texts in this chapter are from the New International Version.

[4] Not long ago a drunken driver going east on the westbound lanes of the Ventura Freeway nearly killed my two children and me. Instead, he caused the death of a family of four in a car behind me. Last night the district attorney flew me home to Los Angeles so I could testify today at the second-degree murder trial. Now I'm typing these words on the plane, flying back east to conclude the Christian life seminar I'm teaching this week.

[5] If you are interested in taking a spiritual gifts inventory of your own talents, write to me and I'll be glad to arrange it. For less than an hour's investment, this fascinating test may tell you much about yourself and your potential that you never knew.

[6] I'll be glad to send you a copy of the *The Desire of Ages* as my gift to you. See if it doesn't warm your heart and inspire you to draw closer to your Saviour.

Chapter 13

Michael Finds a Home

Back in the summer of 1977 the world fell apart for Michael Elias. First he lost his marriage, then his job, and finally the roof over his head. But thanks to God's help, not only has his own life turned around; he has helped thousands of other homeless people put their lives back together.

Michael had been a probation officer for juvenile offenders when his marriage came unraveled. Following the divorce he moved from Maryland to a new life in California. An agency placing professionals in hospitals had asked him to transfer to the West Coast. But by the time he and his two boys arrived in Orange County, the promised job had evaporated.

For the first time in his life Michael found himself unemployed. With meager savings, he couldn't afford an apartment while he searched for work. So there he was, homeless and helpless—and very lonely.

Just at the point of desperation, he heard of Christian Temporary Housing Facility, a struggling year-old ministry about to collapse. Michael moved in with his boys and assumed control of its operation. He had found a home, a job—and a ministry.

CTHF was quite primitive when he took over. It had only sparse furnishings, no phone, and no money. So

Michael organized a committee of local citizens and published a newsletter. Soon furniture and funding began to materialize.

As the ministry expanded he moved CTHF to the city of Orange, where the mayor helped him locate in a vacant home. The county of Orange came through with a grant of $100,000. Then substantial corporate gifts arrived from the Irvine Foundation, the Fluor Corporation, and the Ahamanuson Foundation. Later the United Way became involved as a sponsor.

Many regard Michael's remarkable ministry as a model for helping homeless families. He is so successful that the United States government has become interested. The Department of Housing and Urban Development appointed him to work as a consultant with the United Nations in their recent project Habitat, for homeless people around the world.

I first learned about CTHF while pastoring the Adventist church in nearby Anaheim, wrestling with the problems of homeless families who came to my office begging for help. Frequently we or one of our church families could take them in for a few nights. But then what?

My frustration climaxed one day when yet another rusty low rider chugged up our church driveway. Its cargo of homeless refugees stumbled into my office. Obviously they hadn't bathed in many days. Soon they would be back again, wanting more help.

What should we do about the homeless? I couldn't ignore them, hoping they would go away. They needed an apartment and employment. But suppose they couldn't hold a job? Or what if they just didn't want to work? Did my church owe the help they requested just so they could waste their lives away?

In the light of Christ's instruction in Matthew 25, I obviously had to find some kind of solution. I resolved to get acquainted with others in Orange County who wanted to help the homeless. That's when I met Michael, who already had his fantastic ministry running successfully. He was looking for a local church with which to join forces.

So our church board invited Michael to link up his ministry with our Community Services program. To my delight he accepted our invitation and became our volunteer Community Services leader.

How does he care for the homeless? First, he refuses to lump them all into one vast group. They include the mentally ill, homeless, single people, runaway youth, battered wives with their children, and unemployed families.

Michael specializes in helping homeless families. Many people around the country who lose their employment chase the California dream to Orange County. Instead of landing a new life there, they to their shock find themselves worse off than before. Mammoth housing costs pile on top of the demand for first and last month's rent. Without money and friends or family to help, many homeless families live in their cars or in parks.

It seems a hopeless dilemma. Because they have no permanent address, nobody will hire them. Yet without a job, they can't raise the money to afford a permanent address. That's where Michael Elias and Christian Temporary Housing steps in.

CTHF provides a warm homelike setting for families to reconstruct their lives. To restore their sense of dignity, clients actually operate the shelter—cooking, vacuuming, mowing the lawn—performing the same tasks as if they were home. Michael also helps them find a job. And once employed, they must pay room and board. At the same time they can save some of their earnings to launch out on their own.

But what if they don't want to work? Michael acknowledges the existence of incurably lazy street people, those mentally and physically fit to work but who won't. Michael declines to indulge their indolence. "They have chosen to live outside the laws of society and biblical principles by refusing to work. To pamper them is immoral and illegal, just like condoning prostitution."

However, he quickly adds that very few who are able to support their families are unwilling—given a solid opportunity. He insists that none of his clients have ever refused to work.

In my association with Michael, I have found him tenderhearted, yet never one to let others manipulate him. How does he guard against being taken advantage of? When suspicious, he requests some kind of proof to back up the story. Doctor's papers, perhaps, various forms of identification, and so on. If prospective clients claim to have lost evidence, he offers to help them call for duplicates. If they say they have been robbed, Michael requires a police report of their lost goods.

Thus he manages to weed out phonies before they check into CTHF. Families in genuine need eagerly furnish evidence to prove it. And once in the program, they happily accept whatever employment opens up. Michael is proud of his clients. Incredibly, none has ever robbed him in all his years at CTHF.

God is opening many new doors to his ministry. He heads the Christian Neighbor Program at his church in Anaheim, coordinating 300 volunteers who help needy senior citizens. Along with opening another CTHF facility in Orange County, he has just established the largest shelter for homeless families in the Los Angeles area, Rio Hondo Temporary Home.

Rio Hondo is a model of volunteer forces, business, and government working together. City and state funds support the project with grants, also providing a beautiful building —for the grand sum of a dollar a month!

Michael has grand plans for the future. He wants to set up a national toll-free hotline for the homeless. Phone operators would conduct a thorough interview, determine the need, and refer clients to a suitable local facility.

At the moment, he is discussing the possibilities of working with the Seventh-day Adventist Church to establish a nationwide network of "Good Samaritan Clubs" for housing homeless families. Each club will consist of 10 concerned citizens, church members as well as other interested citizens. After each homeless family has gone through a thorough interview, plans call for them to be placed in an apartment provided by the Good Samaritans. The club will then make intensive efforts to help them find employment.

During the first month the club would pay the total rent for the family. In the second month the family takes care of half the rent from its new employment income. The third month they pay 75 percent. And by the fourth month the family is on its own, once again productive members of society.

The Good Samaritan program would offer homeless families the only chance they may ever have to get back on their feet. And Michael's plan would benefit the rest of us too. No longer need we feel helpless about relieving homeless families. We can make a difference, can get involved in bringing help, and thus provide long-term healing too.

Who knows whether we ourselves might someday lose our homes? Most American families live frighteningly close to bankruptcy—just a couple paychecks away, in fact. If you are strung out on debt and short on savings, you may be a candidate to join the ranks of the homeless. Losing your job could put your family out on the streets faster than you might imagine.

When we find ourselves spending more than we earn, sooner or later judgment day must come. Therefore it seems we would be smart either to increase our income or to decrease our expenses.

Increasing income might mean overworking ourselves, and in the process ruining our health and family life. Consequently, it might be more prudent to discipline our spending. That old saying cannot be overworked: "A penny saved is a penny earned."

Here's a financial efficiency test we might run on ourselves: track every dollar spent from the next couple of paychecks. That way we learn where the leaks might be so we can plug them. Then we can stop asking where the money went—and start telling it where to go.

This means financial planning. First of all, we must set goals. Besides the obvious need to keep our family fed and housed, other goals deserve consideration, such as getting out of debt, owning a home, saving for the education of our children, preparing for retirement.

Without question, escaping the trap of indebtedness should be near the top of our list. Interest expense on our debts is money down the drain—we can't even claim it as a tax deduction anymore.

Some advisers recommend avoiding all debt except for buying a house. That's preferable but perhaps not always possible. When I was first hired as a poor young pastor, for instance, I desperately needed a different car. One day on my way to a ministers' meeting the fuel pump on the old VW took an unscheduled sabbatical. Every 15 minutes I had to pour cold water on it to coax it back to work. Driving along a mountain road beside a river, I had access to all the cold water I needed. No problem there, but alas, I didn't have anything to carry the water back to the car. Finally, in answer to prayer, I located some discarded beer bottles and put them to better use than they had known before.

By that time I was running late. Afraid my tardiness wouldn't make a good impression on my new peers, I hurriedly cast the empty bottles behind my seat and hit the road. I made it to the meeting on time, but . . . later that day I noticed some ministers clustered around my car, peering inside at my beer bottles. I had some fancy explaining to do, believe me. (Never afterward have they let me forget it.) After that narrow escape I thought I'd better borrow some money and buy another car before I found myself out of a job.

Yes, at times we may have no option except to purchase on credit. But except for a home mortgage and possibly a car, borrowing can open the door to trouble. You don't need me to lecture you about those deadly slivers of plastic known as credit cards. Many families have found it necessary to cut them up, burn them, or otherwise destroy them. Others can carry their Visa or MasterCard without using it except in an emergency.

An emergency, by the way, is only when amber, red, or blue lights are flashing—not when K Mart has a one-day special on fishing poles.

So put your debts on a diet, will you? You can't afford any extra burden on your paycheck—or your marriage!

Suppose, however, you find yourself already trapped in financial trouble. The creditors call you day and night until the phone company cuts off service. Then they embarrass you at work. Well, you can't get away from them. So why not propose to them a payoff schedule you can handle, even if it's only $10 a month? Just knowing you've got a financial plan in operation will probably satisfy them and bring you great relief too.

If you need help in financial planning, qualified counselors will volunteer their help. You can call the United Way for a referral. A financial counselor will immediately organize your expenses into a budget. Such a spending plan keeps us focused on our financial goals so we won't cheat ourselves and our families. It's as simple as A, B, C—the same priority scale that helped us in time management a few pages back:

A—Absolutely essential expenditures for immediate needs: food, housing, medical care, transportation to work, bills due. And yes, better not forget taxes. Essential expenditures are basic nonnegotiables without which we would suffer or be sued.

B—Beneficial expenditures that make life more comfortable or provide for the family's long-term need: savings, liquidating debt not immediately due, extra clothing, vacations, basic furnishings.*

You can include in category B reasonable supplements to the bare necessities allowed in category A. Things like butter on the bread (better make that lite margarine), buying a house rather than renting, a more reliable car, or a night out with your spouse and/or kids.

Since the best things in life are free, we don't need to spend lots of money to have fun with our families. One evening each week I take either of my kids, Steve or Christi, down to the beach. We build a little fire together and chase the waves, feed the sea gulls, and just talk. All this doesn't cost much money, yet it enriches our week immeasurably. One other evening my wife and I go out. If we can't afford our favorite vegetarian restaurant, we indulge in frozen yogurt and go window shopping.

Whatever we do together depends upon the priorities set by our budget. We don't usually spend a dime on category B until we have taken care of everything in A. On those occasions when category B is in line, we can happily move on to C:

C—Cravings that aren't sinful extravagance. Such a legitimate wish list might include a new car, replacements for the cat-scratched furniture, or a larger house with an extra bedroom. Maybe even a family trip to the Holy Land someday. That would be nice.

Here is where individual conscience comes in. I have no problem driving a new Toyota Camry with its reliability and room for my kids and long legs—but I'd feel guilty owning certain other cars, even if I could afford them. Whatever my convictions, I pray that God will keep me from condemning Christians who do drive bigger cars than mine. I have no business judging them. A condemning, resentful attitude is no less a sin than greed.

Most of my friends have more time than money. For some of them, though, it's the other way around. They must organize their budget accordingly to accommodate their tight schedules.

One of them with a thriving home business needed a new desk. Not wanting to waste money purchasing something new, he scanned the classifieds and drove around looking for decent used furniture. At last he realized that he was wasting time in this particular case and that it was better for him to buy his desk from a discount store. Even though he had to spend more money than he had hoped, his time was valuable too.

Busy pastors and salespeople who work 14 hours a day and drive 3,000 miles a month can't afford the bother it may take to keep an old car running. They need a newer car they can trust. Also, professionals like physicians, teachers, office workers, and pastors have to maintain a certain standard demanded by their vocation. For instance, they must invest in quality clothes, whether they like it or not, or their credibility suffers. Contractors and "blue collar" workers may need tools and trucks that others don't need.

Here's the point: Not everyone faces the same financial burdens or privileges. So none can judge another—only God can do that. And, according to the Bible, He does expect those who enjoy income beyond their basic needs to fulfill their social and spiritual responsibility: to "contribute to the needs of others."

People of the world may hoard God's gifts for themselves, but the Lord has a higher standard for His people. Remember, whatever advantage we have—whether it be our finances, education, trade skills, extra time available, or whatever—every blessing we have makes us the servant of those who lack. People helping people—that's the Bible way.

Methodist founder John Wesley expressed a rule that said, in effect: *Earn* all you can, then *save* all you can, so you can *give* all you can. Wesley knew nothing of the quick-fix lottery jackpot so many today fruitlessly fantasize about.

It takes discipline to get our finances in order. Many Christians confuse such discipline with legalism. Not necessarily. The determining factor is our motives. Why are we disciplining ourselves? To appease God and do penance for our sins? That would be legalism. But if we in the joy of salvation deny ourselves for the good of God, for others, or for our own real good, that's not legalism at all. It's love, wouldn't you say?

Jesus said: "Where your treasure is, there your heart will be also." "But seek first the kingdom of God and His righteousness, and all these things shall be added to you" (Matthew 6:21, 33).

Putting God first in our lives means placing Him first in our finances, too—and doing so ensures our own stability. In other words, keeping God first keeps us first. Sadly, though, many Christians treat the Lord as if He were the family dog.

The dog gets the leftovers, you know. People feed themselves first, and then if they have anything left over, they throw it to the dog. And they give the Lord mere leftovers from their paycheck.

Is this the way we want to treat our Creator and Saviour? Throwing Him the leftovers? No, "honor the Lord with your possessions, and with the *first*fruits of all your increase; so your barns will be filled with plenty" (Proverbs 3:9, 10).

Have you noticed that every Scriptural call to financial commitment seems accompanied with an assurance of God's provision for us? And the Bible overflows with warnings to those who did not put God first in their finances.

You may recall Christ's story about the greedy farmer. The man's own needs were well taken care of, and he had even stockpiled for the future. Still he wasn't satisfied. When an unexpected windfall came his way, he decided to hoard it for himself rather than share it. Perhaps he planned to take life easy—eat, drink, and be merry!

Nothing in the story indicates that the man was dishonest in any way. I'm sure he was a well-respected businessman, perhaps a leader in his community. He worked hard for his money, and he could do with it anything he pleased. Or so he thought.

You know what happened: "But God said to him, 'You fool! This night your soul will be required of you; then whose will those things be which you have provided?' So is he who lays up treasure for himself, and is not rich toward God" (Luke 12:20, 21).

This poor rich man wasn't rich toward God. He made a bad investment in hoarding his surplus, and his greed cost him his life. Apparently he had forgotten the reason why the Lord had blessed his labors so abundantly. Not so that he might stash it away for himself, but rather so he could share.

In Bible times the top 10 percent of one's profits, the tithe, went directly to God's house: " 'Bring all the tithes into the storehouse, that there may be food in My house, and prove Me now in this,' says the Lord of hosts, 'if I will not open for you the windows of heaven and pour out for you such blessing that there will not be room enough to receive it' " (Malachi 3:10).

Some shun tithepaying as a legalistic leftover from Moses on Mount Sinai. Actually, it is a common-sense principle of financial management that we can trace to Abraham, the pioneer of our faith covenant with God.

In addition to tithe, the Lord asks for offerings, too, as we feel able to give. Tithe would be an A priority, right at the top of that list of absolute essentials. Now, offerings are just as essential, but the amount of offerings we can give could be classed in category B.

Is God expecting too much of us with our tithes and offerings? Not when we consider what He has done on our behalf. Our financial commitment to Him but faintly reflects His gift to us in Christ.

Jesus, you recall, had been rich with the treasures of heaven. He enjoyed wealth we can't even imagine, yet He laid it all aside, coming to earth as the poorest of the human family. And why did He live and die among us? So He could offer us a sound investment—eternal riches in heaven through His free gift of grace which we accept by faith.

Saving faith that responds to Calvary involves commitment. Appreciating what God has done for us, we surrender everything we have and everything we are at the cross of our salvation. And when we dedicate ourselves—with our possessions—to God, He has a surprise for us. He makes us "joint-heirs with Christ" so that everything Jesus owns belongs to us too. As Christians, we "inherit all things" for eternity (Romans 8:17; Revelation 21:7).

Do you realize that you are eternally rich in Christ? As rich as He is in everything? Of course, it may not seem that way right now—God knows that in our world of temptation we are better off without too many possessions to distract us. So He holds most of our wealth in trust until Jesus comes.

Christ's disciples understood all this. They knew more about good financial management than most economists

today. Notice an interesting conversation about invest-
ments that the apostle Peter had with Jesus:

"Peter began to say to Him, 'Behold, we have left
everything and followed You.' Jesus said, 'Truly I say to you,
there is no one who has left house or brothers or sisters or
mother or father or children or farms, for My sake and for
the gospel's sake, but that he shall receive a hundred times
as much now in the present age . . . along with persecutions;
and in the age to come, eternal life. But many who are first,
will be last; and the last, first' " (Mark 10:28-31, NASB).

Did you catch that—a hundredfold return from our
investment! That figures out to 10,000 percent interest
accrued to us right now in this world. Not necessarily in the
form of material wealth. Probably not, in fact. Rather, a
wealth of God's loving-kindness, peace of mind, and the
assurance of His salvation. Ten thousand percent interest
right now, plus eternal life later.

Forget the lottery jackpot—here is something sure,
something certain! I can't find any bankers or brokers who
offer anything close to what God has guaranteed, not to
mention eternal life.

Can you see what the Lord wants to do for us? How can
we help but invest our lives into His love?

If you want more:
Malachi 3:8
Matthew 6:19, 20
2 Corinthians 8:9
2 Corinthians 9:6-8
1 Timothy 6:10

---

*Some might protest placing savings in category B rather than A. Certainly we
should try to set aside savings from every paycheck, once we have paid off high-
interest bills. But if your utilities are about to be disconnected, you had better use
your money to pay the overdue bills rather than putting it in the bank.

Chapter 14

Joy Triumphs Over Tragedy

I'd like you to meet two friends of mine, George and Joy Swift. God turned incredible tragedy into triumph for them. Their journey from death to a new life will bring you hope in facing whatever your future holds.

Their story takes us back to the year 1977. George and Joy had made their escape from big city life and moved to Lake of the Ozarks, a Missouri recreation community. The Swift family included 14-year-old Steve, 12-year-old Greg, the toddler Tonya, and baby Stacy—plus Stephanie, 17, when she came to visit.

Things were kind of crowded in their two-bedroom house. But where there's love, there's room, Joy says. All except the two youngest were George's from his previous marriage. That made no difference to her, who cherished them all the same. They were one big happy family there in that little home.

Then tragedy struck suddenly on September 15, 1977. The day started out normally enough. Morning and afternoon passed along as usual. That evening George and Joy went to the local American Legion Hall for a night out together.

About 10:00 a strange man summoned George outside. Joy followed. A dozen people were milling around, quite agitated, some of them crying.

"What's wrong?" she demanded.

The only answer she could get was "Something terrible happened! Please—just go home!"

So the Swifts jumped into their car and sped to their house. Three miles away they could see across the lake to where their house stood on the hill. The whole hillside was flashing red with emergency lights. A roadblock barred the way to their home.

George and Joy jumped out, only to have ambulance attendants restrain them. "Let me go!" Joy yelled. "Those are my kids in there." But the attendants held them securely. George broke loose, only to be stopped on the porch by two policemen who refused to let him go inside.

The house was dark with one curtain propped open. Joy tried to peer inside as the attendants pulled her toward the ambulance and forced her to sit down.

"What happened?" she was pleading now.

"We don't know," the attendant answered evasively.

"Where are my kids? Are they here in the ambulance?" She turned around and looked, but it was empty.

Finally the attendant ventured softly, "They're still in the house."

Joy glanced again at the pitch black house. Nobody was trying to help her children. Why were they in there alone?

Finally the horrible truth dawned on her. "They're all dead, aren't they?" she whispered.

The attendant nodded.

In the next split second the bottom dropped out of her heart. She sobbed silently as the police put her with her husband in the patrol car and drove them down to the station for questioning.

After four hours of interrogating George, they took Joy in about 4:00 a.m. She doesn't remember much of what they asked her during the next three hours, except that questions about a neighborhood boy by the name of Billy kept coming up. [1]

She cringed at their mention of him. The first day the boys had brought him home, she had a bad impression of him. The 14-year-old seemed obsessed with violence, having a special fascination for guns. He always wanted to get his hands on the pistol George kept from his years as a police officer.

Just two days before, Billy had gotten off the school bus and played with Greg at the house. Joy noticed he was acting kind of strange, as if something were churning in his mind.

The night before the murders George wasn't home. He had visited his oldest daughter, Stephanie, who was in the hospital with ovarian cancer. Joy and the kids heard a knock on the door. It was Billy. He stepped inside and stood there staring at them. At last he left.

Things seemed eerie that night after she put the kids to bed. The dogs outside barked incessantly as the wind wailed in the trees. Joy wondered whether someone might be lurking out there.

When her husband came home after midnight, she told him how strange she had felt all evening. He said it was just her imagination. But she had a hard time getting to sleep that night.

The next day, Thursday, it happened. Joy and George went from loving parents to childless murder suspects, all in the space of a few short hours.

Following the long night of interrogation, the police satisfied themselves that the couple hadn't killed the children, and put the brokenhearted couple up in a motel. That next evening a deputy came over to announce that they had arrested two suspects: a juvenile named Billy and a 20-year-old possible accomplice. The Swifts had no doubt that the boy had indeed committed the crime.

That night the television newscasts carried their story. So did the papers in St. Louis and Kansas City. Tragically, before the Swifts could get to Stephanie in the hospital, she heard on the TV about what had happened to her brothers and sisters. The shock was too much for the girl to bear. Less than three weeks later, Stephanie died from her cancer.

We can only imagine the horror of such an experience. George and Joy groped for answers but couldn't find them. Barricaded at the motel, Joy kept wondering where her children were. In heaven? Someplace else? When would she see them again? She just had to learn the truth about life after death.

Needing to be alone with God, she retreated to an empty room. As she sat there facing the wall, she felt as if the darkness were going to suffocate her. She felt empty and hollow inside. "God, please, God—hear me!" she kept crying.

Nothing but silence. She kept praying. "Please, God. I can't live without my kids. Bring them back—please, God, please!"

Then something happened. Joy began to feel warm and secure. A voice seemed to say, "You don't have to lose them. They are in My hands, and I am with you. I will give you My strength."

All of a sudden it felt as if all the kids were sitting in her lap. Her arms caressed the darkness around her, imagining herself touching and holding the children.

Slowly and peacefully the feeling faded away. The voice seemed to tell her, "You'll be with them again. You're separated from them only for a little while. The answers you seek I will show you in My Book."

As she rose from that corner she was a changed person. She knew God was with her, that she didn't have to fight life's battle alone. Walking quietly back to the bed, she pulled the Bible out of the desk and reverently opened its pages. There she found strength to face the funeral service and the court proceedings.

The juvenile court waived jurisdiction over Billy, which meant he would face trial as an adult on four counts of murder. That was important to the Swifts, for now they saw a chance he might be punished for his crime. The authorities also filed four counts of murder against Ray, the 20-year-old.

Although Billy forfeited his right to a jury trial, he managed to arrange a plea bargain with the Johnson County Circuit Court. Even so, the judge sentenced him to spend the rest of his life in prison.

Ray, who had driven Billy to the crime and helped him in the murders, pleaded not guilty by reason of mental defect. He was a weak-minded individual, easily influenced. The crime was Billy's idea, Ray insisted; he only went along with it.

The jury found Ray guilty of two counts of second-degree murder and gave him a light sentence. That upset the Swifts, as you might understand. They didn't see any justice in the verdict.

Gradually, however, Joy's resentment healed as her relationship with Jesus deepened. She came to realize that Christ died for all of us, even murderers. And He prayed for His own murderers, "Father, forgive them." She concluded that just as God had forgiven her sins through Christ, Billy and Ray had a right to forgiveness too. Maybe someday they might even decide to repent and be saved!

As time passed and God healed their wounds, the Swifts were able to look toward the future. They decided to start a new family. Before long, little Sandy came along to replenish their lives. Soon Matthew Thomas showed up, followed not long after by Michael George.

Meanwhile, God kept His promise and gave Joy the answers she needed about death and the resurrection. She met a nurse who one day found her looking at pictures of her murdered children, tears rolling down her face. The nurse sat beside her and admired the pictures. Thankful for a compassionate friend, Joy shared the story about that night in the motel room when she cowered in the corner calling out to God.

The nurse listened intently until Joy had finished pouring out her heart. "I'm a Seventh-day Adventist Christian," the woman said finally, "and I believe Jesus is coming again very soon. And when He does, you'll see your children again. The Bible says, 'Seek and ye shall find.' You'll find your answers, believe me. I'm here anytime you need to talk—and I've got a shoulder you can cry on, too."

The nurse left her with the picture sitting beside her and the Bible open in her hands. Hope filled her heart again, along with a burning desire to discover in the Scriptures more about Christ's coming so she could be with her kids again.

Holding the Bible in her lap, Joy thought, *This Book has everything: how to raise your kids, how to be a good wife, how to treat others, what is best to eat, standards of living, prophecies—and most of all love, hope, and wisdom. What a terrific Book! Why haven't I read it before?*

But now things were different in her life. She would seek, and she would find the answers. Meanwhile, her sister Dawn had also been searching for the truth about life and death. She received a card offering free study-by-mail Bible guides from the Voice of Prophecy. The Bible was the only textbook, leading her along one subject at a time. Dawn found her answers and felt she had to share them with Joy. [2]

One day she approached her sister and asked, "Do you believe your kids are in heaven, or sleeping in the grave until Jesus comes?"

"I don't know, Dawn. Someone in my church once told me that Tonya and Stacy were in limbo because they hadn't been baptized. But I can't believe God would do that to them. I'd much rather believe they were asleep, waiting for me to go with them to heaven when Jesus comes."

"There is no limbo in the Bible," Dawn explained. "In fact, the Bible says that the dead know not anything. When people die they simply cease to exist, and their body returns to dust, awaiting either the resurrection of life or the resurrection of judgment."

When Dawn showed her those things right in the Bible, the truth set her free. Joy also learned the real meaning of baptism, discovering that the Bible nowhere mentions infants being baptized. Instead, Scripture says, "He who has believed and has been baptized shall be saved" (Mark 16:16, NASB).

So baptism is important to the salvation response, but not for babies—since they cannot believe. What parents did in New Testament times was to dedicate their infants to God. Then their children would make their own decisions as to whether they wanted to be baptized, after they were old enough to believe in Jesus for themselves.

Joy also discovered that the word *baptism* means "to submerge, to immerse." "As soon as Jesus was baptized, He went up out of the water," Matthew 3:16 declares (NIV). Notice that Jesus rose up out of the water after His baptism. He had not been sprinkled or poured upon. Rather He was submerged, immersed into the Jordan River. Believers in Christ are "buried with him in baptism," says the apostle Paul (Colossians 2:12).

She learned that getting baptized is similar to getting married. Just like a wedding, baptism is a public ceremony of commitment. Two thousand years ago Jesus gave His life to us. Now it's our opportunity to turn our lives over to Him. Baptism signifies and celebrates this union of ourselves with Jesus.

Deeply appreciating what Jesus meant to her, Joy couldn't hold herself back from a total surrender to Him. She began attending church every Sabbath and before long announced to George her decision to be baptized and join the Adventist family of believers.

At first her husband didn't appreciate her convictions. Considering his wife's new beliefs a threat to their togetherness, he opposed her. Normally she followed his wishes, but not in this case. She realized that Jesus, not George, had created her and redeemed her. God had to come first in her life, even before her marriage. So she went ahead with her baptism, even at the risk of alienating her husband.

As time went on, however, George found himself attracted toward her new experience. Sabbath came to be the happiest day of the week for all of them, as together they entered God's rest. The turning point in his decision for Christ came in April 1987. That's when the Swift family flew out to California to tape a telecast for *It Is Written*, the ministry for which I do script writing and prayer counseling. We needed to have the Swifts with us only a day or two for the taping, but I arranged for them to be with us a whole week. I confess it was a little scheme between Joy and me, in the hope that we might be able to encourage George in his relationship with Christ.

During that week he enjoyed fellowship with many telecast staff members. He also discussed questions on his mind with a number of us, including *It Is Written* speaker George Vandeman. At the end of the week George Swift dropped a real surprise on us. He announced that he had decided to surrender his life to Jesus and be baptized.

You should have seen the look of joy on Joy's face! All of us erupted in celebration.

Afterward I asked him what had influenced him to take his stand. Pastor Vandeman's kindly counsel was an important factor, certainly. And something my wife said sealed the decision. It happened when we emerged from our cars after returning from Disneyland. While I was teasing the kids, Darlene felt impressed to turn to George and say, "You know, you don't have to be perfect to be baptized. Jesus is your perfection. All you need is to be willing to give your life to Him!"

He thought it over and decided it made sense. And so he made the big decision.

After the Swifts flew home, they asked for Bible studies from a local pastor, Terry Darnall. Later that summer, on a beautiful sunny afternoon, a little group of singing believers watched the pastor lower George into the cool, clear waters of the Bitterroot River. He came up dripping with happiness.

George and Joy are closer now than ever, thanks to their mutual faith in Christ and their new church fellowship. They tell their thrilling story to eager audiences of thousands around North America. And when they aren't out traveling, they teach the children's Sabbath school in their little home church there in the Rocky Mountains.

How about you and me? Are we willing to take our stand for Jesus like Joy and George did?

Human nature tends to delay—you know how it is every morning when that alarm rings. Often we even postpone getting around to something we really want to do.

It's much easier to float downstream like a dead fish than to swim against the current—even when we really want to be upstream. The essence of maturity is disciplining ourselves to pass up the easy way for a higher long-term good. Any Olympic athlete will testify to that.

Sometimes we have to forgo a ball game for the sake of finally getting the garage cleaned out. We forsake a window shopping trip to the mall to tackle that dirty oven. Not much fun to start with, but the rewards are well worth whatever trouble it takes to do what needs to be done. And if that is true with household chores, how much more rewarding when it comes to following Jesus!

Back in the first century Peter and his brother Andrew were going about their business one day when all of a sudden Jesus came along with an inconvenient invitation: "Follow Me." You can imagine the excuses they might have come up with. Instead, "they immediately left the nets and followed Him" (Mark 1:18, NASB).

Nothing could stop them from going with Jesus. And they did it right away.

Christ today invites us, as well, to abandon our old ways and follow completely all the light shining from His Word.

Why wait?

If you want more:
    Acts 8:35-38
    Acts 14:19-22
    Acts 16:16-33
    Acts 22:16
    2 Corinthians 6:2

----

[1] To get the full story, you must read Joy Swift's best-selling book, *They're All Dead, Aren't They.* Joy has also authored another book, on grief recovery: *Goodbyes Aren't Forever.*

[2] I know the people at the Voice of Prophecy very well, since I used to work there. Let me tell you that their New Life Bible Course is the finest study-by-mail guide available anywhere. And it is free. The same Bible counselors who helped Joy so much are eager to hear from you. Here's their address: Voice of Prophecy, Box 55, Los Angeles, California 90055. They will send you the first study guide. Look it over, and if you like it, fill it out and they will send you more.

Chapter 15

Willa Tames a Savage

I was a stubborn, stiff-necked, full-blown drug addict," the former master of menace bellowed to his high school audience. "And an alcoholic, too—I drank two gallons of wine a day. Two gallons! Do you realize how much that is?"

The students gasped as the 16-time Pacific Northwest wrestling champion continued. "My habits cost me my family, my health, and all my money. Three million dollars down the drain before I hit rock-bottom.

"That night in 1979 I came home to be welcomed at the door by divorce papers. My children had taken a vote—they wanted me out. My wife made me leave right then. I found myself out on the dark streets with nothing but $71 and my Visa card. And a gun.

"All alone with no one to live for, I loaded the revolver. Then I stuck it between my teeth and pulled the trigger. Nothing happened. I pulled again and still the gun stayed stuck. I was so helpless I couldn't even kill myself!"

It had been a long way down to the bottom of the barrel for Dutch Savage. Born Francis Stewart, Jr., the six-foot-five son of a Pennsylvania coal miner starred as an all-state football player. Later he devoted his intimidating physical skills to the wrestling ring.

His addiction to drugs began one night in Georgia. Desperate to relieve the agony of hobbling around the ring on an injured ankle, he accepted a friend's offer of some pain-killing pills. He never intended to get hooked (who does?).

As his career skyrocketed, he descended deeper into drugs. He bullied his way to *Ring Wrestling* magazine's International Championship title, as well as becoming the many-time champion of the Pacific Northwest.

Without question 270-pound Dutch dished out more pain than he got back, yet he suffered plenty of punishment. He reports with a rueful smile, "My ankles have been broken and my elbows, too. I have no kneecaps. I've broken my shinbones and thighbones. My shoulders and joints have all been dislocated. I've had 32 concussions . . ." The list goes on mercilessly.

With the pain came an ever-increasing drug dependency. Cocaine, opium, heroin, you name it. "I popped everything I could find and didn't even get a buzz," he recalls. Dutch also drowned himself in alcohol to quench his pain.

The pain he suffered went deeper than his physical injuries. Despite all the money and fame, his whole life was one big ball of agony. Right down to the depths of his soul. Misery was his only companion.

The night he couldn't kill himself was the same night he finally found God. Actually, it was God who finally got through to him.

Desperate for someone who could help him, Dutch grabbed a phone book and searched for the name of a pastor. Then he jumped in his truck and raced through the streets of Vancouver, Washington, searching wildly for the pastor's house. There he welcomed Jesus into his life.

Dutch gained an immediate victory over a quarter century of alcoholism, but his struggle with narcotics persisted for the next two years. He seemed to be missing something spiritually. What could it be?

For two years he searched in vain. Although he counseled with many pastors, nothing he heard satisfied the strange spiritual hunger within him. Then one day at a shopping mall Dutch met the woman God used to help him find fulfillment in his relationship with Jesus. Willa was leaving the Sears store as Dutch came in. She recognized him from his television appearances. They quickly fell in love.

Night after night driving back from wrestling matches, Willa noticed Dutch pulling out a plastic bag filled with various drugs. He would tear open the bag, grab a handful of pills, and gulp them down. He also indulged from his large cache of marijuana.

Although Willa at the time was still backslidden spiritually, she didn't like his drug abuse. Dutch also became verbally abusive. It got so bad she had to tell him goodbye.

That shook him up. So much so that he pledged, with God's help, he would never touch drugs again. Kneeling, he prayed, "Lord, I'll do my part by taking the first step in putting these drugs down. But You've got to help me leave them there."

Dutch has never since touched narcotics.

Only one addiction remained to chain his soul—tobacco. Every day he consumed three or four pouches of Red Man chew. Finally he conquered it after a youth group asked him to tell them his life story. A Christian friend, Al, confronted him several days before he was to speak. "Dutch, how can you stand in front of those teenagers and urge them to let Jesus change their lives when you're still fooling around with that filthy stuff?"

Angry, he kept chewing, that day and the next. Then the third day the Holy Spirit caught up with him. Dutch humbled himself and admitted to Willa, "Al's absolutely right!" He announced to the teens his decision to quit.

From that day to this, he has never again used tobacco.

God was doing wonderful things for Dutch and Willa. One afternoon a Seventh-day Adventist pastor showed up at the Savage home. His visit brought the spiritual guidance Dutch had been longing for.

At first he couldn't understand the Sabbath. It seemed so strange! But rather than rejecting it or ignoring it, he determined to study it out. With Willa's encouragement, he took his stand for the Sabbath. It was one more step with

Jesus. He had already accepted Christ as Saviour and Lord of his life. It was only natural now to worship Jesus as Lord of the Sabbath. He and Willa celebrated their new relationship with Christ by getting baptized. And married.

Dutch's favorite day of the week is Sabbath. Every week he finds himself refreshed by entering Sabbath rest in Christ as His Saviour and Creator. Of course, he doesn't restrict his relationship with Jesus to the seventh day. Every day he faithfully studies his Bible and sets aside special time for prayer.

He and Willa enjoy the closest of relationships. Dutch wants everyone to know how God used her to enrich his life. He even requested her name in the title of this chapter—"Willa Tames a Savage."

Thanks to Jesus his Saviour and Willa his wife, Dutch's life is now complete. You see, he has changed arenas now, from the wrestling ring to a battlefield even more treacherous and rewarding—the war against narcotics and alcohol.

In cooperation with the Adventist Church, Dutch heads Northwest Outreach. It's a self-supporting, nonprofit ministry staffed by doctors and counselors, along with athletes who overcame their addiction. Working through local law enforcement agencies, N.O. encounters students ranging from lower elementary to high school. Thousands have signed a covenant to rid their lives of drugs forever, with the help of God. Each respondent receives the teen journal *Listen*, acclaimed by many educators as the best tool available for ongoing narcotics education.

Dutch's program works. He commands attention with his huge physique and booming voice. Despite his intimidating presence, the kids can sense he cares about them, and his love strikes home to their hearts.

One high school principal observed, "Dutch Savage has a certain charisma and genuineness about him that causes students to open up, be honest, and listen." And a teacher expressed her appreciation with the words, "Your love and concern radiated in your message."

From an anguished and abusive addict God has changed him to a loving and lovable believer.

Despite his continuing popularity, Dutch is a humble man. Churches of many denominations invite him to their pulpits. Recently his ministry expanded to college campuses as well as to Oregon State Penitentiary. "I'm not ashamed to tell anyone what Christ has done for me," he declares.

Can you imagine where he might be now if he had refused to abandon his former life for the sake of new life in Jesus?

It wasn't easy for Dutch to change. His struggle reminds me of some of my fellow writers, who are reluctant to exchange outdated equipment for the blessing of a computer. Although they could afford to make the switch, they feel comfortable with their old Selectrics. Thus they remain in the confines of their old cocoon.

It's a high price they pay for refusing to stretch their wings. If they only knew the joy and freedom of new opportunity . . .

I thank God for the day I saw that computer ad in *Time* magazine. For the first time I realized what computers could do to change my life. Naturally, I felt an attachment to my old, comfortable way of writing. And yes, when I changed over I did suffer a couple weeks of disorientation. But after those first few days of uncertainty my professional life has been transformed forever. To think, I almost resisted . . .

No, it's not easy to leave the comfort of familiar paths and accept something new—whether it be computer technology or Bible truth. Somehow it seems that by obeying God we would be throwing our lives away. Maybe that is why Jesus left us the warning and the promise "For whoever desires to save his life will lose it, but whoever loses his life for My sake will save it" (Luke 9:24).

How is it with you and me? Is it possible there may be advanced light for us to follow? Neglected truths from God's Word we need to obey today—whatever our denominational background? The Bible says, "But the path of the just is like the shining sun, that shines ever brighter unto the perfect day" (Proverbs 4:18).

But so many seem reluctant to welcome new light. You may have heard of the Flat Earth Research Society. The members have convinced themselves that our world is not shaped like a ball but rather like a platter. You can even hear them arguing on radio talk shows. When shown photographs proving the earth is round, they explain, "It's round like a coin but also flat like a coin."

Somehow they find comfort in believing only what their beloved ancestors taught centuries ago. They refuse to accept the unfolding evidence of science.

I wonder if some Christians today belong to a religious flat earth society. Convinced by the creeds of their ancestors, they are reluctant to move along with the unfolding evidence of Scripture. They lack the spirit of adventure, a willingness to accept new truth from God's Word.

Let me illustrate this point of finding ourselves in losing ourselves for Christ's sake. Suppose one August afternoon you are driving along the Gospel Freeway through Death Valley, California. Hot isn't nearly the word for what you are suffering. Having your windows rolled down doesn't help much.

Then you notice someone hitchhiking out there. Normally you might not want to pick up hitchhikers, but this one looks different. Why, it's Jesus!

Gladly you pull over and welcome the Lord into your car. The two of you are getting acquainted when suddenly He has a strange request. "Would you roll up your window?"

Now, while you want to please Jesus, He does seem to be asking too much here. You haven't been enjoying the way things are in the car, and you've been hoping for relief. But the little comfort you now experience comes from having your window open. And Jesus wants you to forfeit the only thing that makes life bearable? No! Such a request is downright unreasonable.

So you politely decline. "I'd rather not, Lord—if You don't mind. Your commandment would turn my car into an oven."

Then Jesus points to other cars on the freeway whose drivers have their windows rolled up. "They obeyed My commandment, and they look quite happy and comfortable, don't you think?"

"I have to admit they do. I've wondered about those people before, but I always figured there was something different about them. How they can live like that and be happy is beyond me!"

Jesus looks disappointed, but He doesn't give up easily. He gently reminds you how much He loves you. He explains how He died for you and has prepared a home in heaven so you can live with Him eternally.

Then He makes a direct appeal. "In the light of all I've done for you and all I offer you, is it really asking too much for you to close your window? Trust Me—I'll give you an abundant life beyond your imagination."

"Well, Lord, all right! I can't see any reason to roll up the window, but since You sacrificed Your life and saved my sinful soul, the least I can do in gratitude is obey Your commandments."

And so with a brave smile you roll up your window. Then, with a bigger smile than yours, Jesus reaches over and pushes a little blue button you've never noticed before.

Air conditioning! Ah . . . that sudden flow of cool, wonderful air.

You never dreamed that obeying Jesus could be such a pleasant experience. As soon as you surrendered what you had been tempted to hold back, He gave you higher joy and deeper fulfillment than you had dreamed possible. Everything happens when we step out in faith.

When we lose ourselves for Jesus' sake, we find ourselves more fulfilled than we had imagined possible. But if we hold back, we forfeit everything.

If you are a Christian, you already know the truth of what we're talking about. Like me, you may have delayed and dragged your feet about coming to Jesus. Then you finally broke down and accepted Him—and new life in Christ brought such joy and peace, you wonder what took you so long!

Such obedience of faith isn't a one-time act. There are all kinds of windows Jesus wants us to keep rolling up. And He has all kinds of blue buttons we still don't know about.

Yes, we must maintain that decision to lose ourselves for Jesus' sake all life long. Every step of the way, stubborn, doubting human nature resists God's commands (I'm talking about myself here). So Jesus never promised an easy life. But He did assure us an abundant one as we obey His plan for our lives, as we walk in the light of new truth shining from His Word.

Repenting of our sins. Being baptized into Christ. Entering His Sabbath rest. Everything seems so hard at first. Then we remember His invitation and His promise: "Come to Me, all you who labor and are heavy laden, and I will give you rest." "My yoke is easy and My burden is light" (Matthew 11:28, 30).

In the pages of this book you have met some very special people. Willa and Dutch Savage. Joy and George Swift. Michael Elias. Dr. Benjamin Carson. Noble Alexander.

Each of them is different, yet all have so much in common. All have tasted loneliness. All have struggled in their commitment to Christ—and all have overcome their reluctance. They have all been baptized. They all observe the Sabbath.

Believe me, God loves you just as much as He loves them—you are every bit as special. God has designed a unique plan for your life. Would you like to roll up the windows and accept His complete will for you?

Don't wait for some feeling. Just say "Yes!" to Jesus. Faith moves forward *now.*

I don't know what challenges you may be facing at this time. But I do know this: With Jesus in your heart you will enjoy the abundant life He promises. You need be lonely no longer!

The Bible says "God sets the lonely in families" (Psalm 68:6, NIV). A church family, with brothers and sisters with whom you can grow and share—a home for your heart until Jesus comes to take us all to our heavenly home.

Membership in the family of God has responsibilities. But membership also has its privileges.

Is God speaking to your heart now? Why not discuss your convictions and your questions with the friend who gave you this book?

Or write me a letter. Just tell me what's on your heart. I'd love to hear from you, and I want to give you some materials you'll enjoy reading. Here's my address:

Martin Weber
C/o IT IS WRITTEN TELECAST
Box O
Thousand Oaks,
California 91360

If you want more:
Matthew 25:31-34
Luke 9:23-26
John 16:13
Revelation 14:12
Revelation 22